SHAKESPEARE and ENGLISH HISTORY

By W. H. Rogers

About the Author

1. Professor of English, Florida State College for Women and Florida State University, 1922-64. Head of English Department, 1947-1956. Retired June 30, 1964.

2. Education: B. A. Davidson College 1913; M. A. University of Virginia, 1916; Ph.D. University of Virginia, 1922. Litt. D. Davidson College, 1964. Member of Phi Beta Kappa, Omicron Delta Kappa.

3. Publications: Author of A HISTORY OF THE BOOK REVIEW, 1922; THE BEST OF BROWNING, 1941 (Thomas Nelson & Sons: Ronald Press). Articles in various journals and magazines.

About the Book

1. An objective treatment of the historical background of each of the ten historical plays of Shakespeare, followed in each treatment by a resume of the play and the manner in which Shakespeare used historical fact for his dramatic purpose.

2. A careful discussion of the main characters of each of the ten plays.

3. A series of genealogical tables showing the relationship of the various characters to each other.

SHAKESPEARE

and

ENGLISH HISTORY

by

WILLIAM HUDSON ROGERS
PROFESSOR EMERITUS OF ENGLISH,
FLORIDA STATE UNIVERSITY
Tallahassee, Florida

1966

LITTLEFIELD, ADAMS & CO.
Totowa, New Jersey

PR 3014
.R6

Contents

CHAPTER X

CHAPTER XI

CHAPTER XII

TABLES

SHAKESPEARE
and
ENGLISH HISTORY

CHAPTER I

Introduction

The ten historical plays of Shakespeare cover a period in English history of 320 years. Thanks to the great dramatist, this period is more familiar to the average man or woman than any similar reach of years in all English history. The weakness of Henry VI, the baseness of King John, the murderous evil of Richard of Gloucester, the strength of Henry V, the blind assumption of Richard II are all common knowledge to the man who knows nothing of the characters of Charles I, of George II, or even of Victoria. One reads Shakespeare when one does not read history, and the genius of the playwright has delineated ably the times, the character, the personality, the intrigues, the strength and the weakness of his leading characters. Shakespeare's inspired pen has limned indelibly the features of the more prominent personages who lived between the years 1215 and 1533; each character in his plays is a living human being, moving in reality, full-sized and clear; and from the time when the curtain rises on King John receiving Chatillon, the French Ambassador, to the moment when that same curtain rings down on Cranmer's prophecy of Elizabeth's greatness, the pageant of English history is unfolded for us in a manner which has never yet been equalled. It is the genius of Shakespeare that has caused the events of this period to impress themselves so indelibly on the minds of those who read his plays.

The composition of the historical plays was by no means haphazard. There is no doubt that Shakespeare wrote all of his plays for his immediate present, and it is possible that the Bard himself would be most surprised of all to discover that the world revered his name as it does three hundred years after his death. But if he did write for his own time and his own theater, a fact to which so much evidence points, yet it may easily be seen that a very definite scheme runs throughout the series, revealing the more the genius of the man. The plays were not written nor published in chronological order, but in each play there may be found very definite links joining it to the one preceding it historically and to the one immediately following. It is evident that the poet visualized the whole series before he began the first; but it is interesting to know that the first play he wrote was the sixth in historical order. Shakespeare wrote first the Henry VI trilogy (1590-1592); this was followed in 1593 by *Richard III* and *King John*, in 1595 by *Richard II*, in 1597 by *Henry IV*, Part I, and in 1598 by *Henry IV*, Part II, and by *Henry V* in 1599. *Henry VIII*, the last play of his career, he finished in 1612. Yet, if these plays are read in their chronological order, one is never conscious of anything save a smooth movement from one to the other, and one is extremely impressed by the incidents that consciously link the plays together. From reading the plays alone one would never guess that eight of the plays intervene between the writing of *Henry V* and *Henry VI*, Part I; nor that *Henry VI* was written prior to *Henry V*. Shakespeare apparently knew what he was about, before he started.

Then, too, there is an apparent thread of purpose running through the ten plays. Of course, we will never know what Shakespeare himself thought of his creation; it may be that he wrote simply for the box office, and never dreamed that his work would pass down the ages among the world's greatest masterpieces of dramatic art. It may be that he had no other purpose in mind than simply to produce dramas that people of London of his day would go to the theater to see enacted. One often wonders if Shakespeare ever in the deepest recesses of his imagination intended to convey meanings that critics have imputed to him, or entertained all the theories that critics have said he entertained. However that may be, it is easy to observe a line of thought apparently running through these ten plays, an evident purpose in the series. Beginning with John, son of the first Plantagenet, the dramatist has traced the fortunes of the House of Plantagenet from its beginning to its end in the death of Richard III on Bosworth Field. We can see this thread, whether Shakespeare intended it or not. Then, too, there is a second purpose apparent to the close student of the plays: an attempt to show that Feudalism, founded by William the Conqueror, strengthened by his immediate successors, becoming decadent in the days of Richard II, ridiculed in the mock-chivalry of Falstaff, finally peters out in the inglorious end of Richard III and dies a natural death. Still another theme may be observed: the gradual rise into power of the common people, as shown towards the end by the fact that Richard of Gloucester, intent on mounting the throne he himself had recently made vacant by the death of all who stood in his way, took especial pains to court the favor of the commonalty as if his very success depended on their will. These themes are there. Shakespeare may not have consciously intended to insinuate them into his plays; yet it is easy for us to assume that he did.

In historical sequence the plays begin with King John receiving from the French Ambassador the ultimatum of the French King Philip demanding that John relinquish to his nephew Arthur the throne of England. Around this claim of Arthur, in addition to John's quarrel with the Pope, the whole play is centered. Then a leap is made of 180 years through six reigns, and we come to Richard II, son of the Black Prince, whose misrule and arrogance finally cause him to be deposed by his cousin, Henry Bolingbroke. The plays then follow the fortunes of each succeeding reign from Richard II to Richard III, with the one exception of that of Edward IV, and a part of that is included in the play, *Richard III*. Then there is another leap of fifty years, which brings us to the last of the historical plays, *Henry VIII*, the main point of which is the birth of Elizabeth. If we look upon the plays from *Richard II* to *Richard III* as the main body of the series of historical plays, we may consider *King John* the prologue to the series, and *Henry VIII* the epilogue.

Quoting from the German critic, Schlegel: "The dramas derived from the English history, ten in number, form one of the most valuable of Shakespeare's works, and are partly the

fruit of his maturest age. I say advisedly *one* of his works:
for the Poet evidently intended them to form one great whole.
It is, as it were, an historical heroic poem in the dramatic
form, of which the several plays constitute the rhapsodies. The
main features of the events are set forth with such fidelity;
their causes, and even their secret springs, are placed in so
clear a light; that we may gain from them a knowledge of
history in all its truth; while the living picture makes an impression on the imagination which can never be effaced. But
this series of dramas is designed as the vehicle of a much
higher and more general instruction; it furnishes examples of
the political course of the world, applicable to all times. This
mirror of kings should be the manual of princes: from it they
may learn the intrinsic dignity of their hereditary vocation;
but they will also learn the difficulties of their situation, the
dangers of usurpation, the inevitable fall of tyranny, which
buries itself under its attempts to obtain a firmer foundation;
lastly the ruinous consequences of the weaknesses, errors, and
crimes of kings, for whole nations, and many subsequent generations. Eight of these plays, from *Richard II* to *Richard III,*
are linked together in uninterrupted succession, and embrace
a most eventful period of nearly a century of English history.
The events portrayed in them not only follow each other, but
are linked together in the closest and most exact connection;
and the cycle of revolts, parties, civil and foreign wars, which
began with the deposition of Richard II, first ends with the
accession of Henry VII to the throne."

Shakespeare did not at all times adhere closely to historical
fact. His plays are dramatic revivifications of the past, and
when he saw that some deviation from the straight line of
historic truth was necessary for the dramatic effect he desired,
he at no time hesitated to deviate. If it was necessary for the
child-wife of Richard II to conduct herself as a mature woman,
it was so ordered. If dramatic necessities ordained that Arthur
should be a claimant to the throne of England, claimant he
became, even though history tells us that Arthur made no
such claim and that Richard Coeur de Lion expressly willed his
kingdom to his brother John. If it seemed expedient for Hotspur
to be matched throughout with Hal in respect to age and
achievements, Shakespeare did not hesitate to do so, despite

the fact that Hotspur was old enough to be Hal's father. When the Poet makes free with history and varies from the actual order of things it is usually in quest of something higher and more effective than mere historical accuracy; the results in dramatic effect more often than not justified the liberty that he took.

Then, too, there is the fact of Shakespeare's patriotic bias. It must be remembered that the Poet was writing at the age of England's first coming to greatness. The Spanish Armada had been defeated by the English only two years before the appearance of the first of the historical plays. England emerged from that conflict the world's foremost sea-power, and this fact, together with the glamour of Elizabeth's reign, had instilled into the hearts and souls of all Englishmen a patriotic fervor perhaps never since attained. It was a period of tremendous national enthusiasm. Therefore it is not strange that poets and dramatists of the period were vying with each other in high-sounding rhapsodies, glorifying the greatness that had so recently burst over England. Thus we see Henry V at Agincourt defeating the French, himself losing but twenty-nine men while the French losses were ten thousand. Only patriotic blindness could prevent one's seeing the absurdity of such a condition. In the same play we find Henry taunting the French emissary, instructing him to go back to his King and tell him that the English are sick, and in that condition one Englishman is worth only one Frenchman; otherwise, one Englishman was equal to three Frenchmen. This same idea is presented when the overbearing Pistol captures a French soldier and bullies him into fawning suppliance. Shakespeare's treatment of Joan of Arc is another example of his letting his patriotism run away with his sense of values; but the critic of his attitude must take into consideration the fact that Shakespeare was writing less than a hundred years from the days of the Maid of Orleans, at a time when the English hated the French as heartily as they did a hundred years before. It is very difficult to be patriotic and at the same time unbiassed.

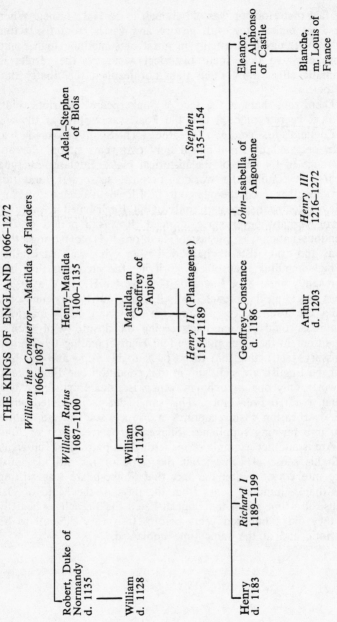

THE KINGS OF ENGLAND 1066-1272

William the Conqueror—Matilda of Flanders
1066–1087

Robert, Duke of Normandy
d. 1135

William
d. 1128

William Rufus
1087–1100

Henry—Matilda
1100–1135

Matilda, m
Geoffrey of
Anjou

William
d. 1120

Adela–Stephen
of Blois

Stephen
1135–1154

Henry II (Plantagenet)
1154–1189

Henry
d. 1183

Richard I
1189–1199

Geoffrey–Constance
d. 1186

Arthur
d. 1203

John–Isabella of Angouleme

Henry III
1216–1272

Eleanor,
m. Alphonso
of Castile

Blanche,
m. Louis of
France

CHAPTER II

Historical Resume from William the Conqueror to King John

October 14, 1066 is one of the truly memorable dates in history. The chronicle of events in England prior to that time has always been more or less in a sort of mist to the average student of affairs; few have cared to read of Egbert, Edgar, Canute, Hardicanute, or of others who reigned as kings in England before the turning of the eleventh century. Of the numerous rulers of that early period only the name of Alfred the Great (871-901), of Edward the Confessor (1042-1066), and of Harold II (1066) are familiar in any manner to the casual mind. But an event occurred in 1066 that changed the whole course of English history; in fact, to many people that date is the beginning of English history.

Edward the Confessor died on January 5, 1066, and was succeeded on the throne by Earl Harold, brother of Edward's wife. In this same year William, duke of Normandy, whose great-aunt Emma was Edward's mother, whose father was Duke Robert of Normandy, and whose mother was Arletta, daughter of a tanner, decided to assert for himself a claim to the throne recently made vacant by the death of the Confessor. William of Normandy was by no means a stranger in England; he had visited in England in the year 1051, and while there he had seen the possibility of acquiring for himself the throne, especially since there was apparently some understanding between him and Edward to that effect. But when Edward died fifteen years later, other claimants seem to have forestalled William, and Harold was chosen king. Therefore, in the same year Wil-

7

liam made ready to punish Harold for such boldness and at the same time to take possession of England, to add it to the holdings of the Norman princes. He had already recently defeated the king of France and in 1063 had annexed the provinces of Anjou and Maine and later Brittany. Because of these victories he was called the Conqueror, before he made his expedition into England.

The result of his expedition is familiar to everyone. He landed in England and met Harold with his forces at Senlac, near Hastings. Harold was defeated and slain. The witanagemot at London formally offered the crown to William, who accepted it without undue hesitation.

Prior to the Norman Conquest England had had very little to do with France; to the Frenchman of that day Englishmen were barbarians, uncultured and uninteresting; no contacts were desired. And on the other side the English had very little intercourse with France save as a place to visit occasionally. The Channel was a natural barrier difficult to cross, and each people dwelt to themselves. But William's coming immediately changed all of that; his conquest of England made it automatically a province of Normandy, or on the other hand, when he became chief of Normandy, the province of Normandy become the property of the king of England. From that time forward for four hundred years the crown of England had rights of ownership in parts of France, rights that frequently were protested by means of arms; for four hundred years scarcely a king ascended the English throne who did not at some time or other find it necessary to invade France in order to sustain the English claim to certain French provinces; nearly all English expeditions into France from Henry I to Henry VI have their origin in the Norman Conquest. King John almost succeeded in losing everything in France that England could lay claim to, but it remained for Henry VI finally and for all time to suffer the loss of all that had been acquired by his illustrious ancestors of the Plantagenets and Normans; and it is to the weakness of Henry VI that England today owes its greatness, for so long as England was hampered by continental holdings she never had a chance to materialize into the great power she became immediately after Henry VI, under the guidance of the Tudors.

So William the Conqueror established the Norman line of kings on the throne of England. Upon his accession, king by right of conquest and election of the witanagemot, he undertook to strengthen his position. He built castles, gave land grants, created earldoms, established a church, issued the Doomsday Book (1086), and organized the principles of feudalism that held firmly in England for so long a time. Then in 1087, while in France on an expedition of revenge, having just burnt the little town of Nantes-sur-Seine in retaliation for a coarse joke played on him by the French king, Phillip I, his horse stumbled, having shied from stepping on some burning embers. William was injured so badly that after lingering six weeks he died.

Upon the Conqueror's death his oldest son, Robert, became duke of Normandy, and the second son, William Rufus, became king of England. Perhaps the one outstanding event of the reign of William Rufus was the First Crusade, in 1099, resulting in the capture of Jerusalem from the Seljukian Turks. The chief result of this event was a spread of a European feeling among the hitherto disconnected countries of Europe; the raising of the whole standard of Western civilization by a taste of the luxuries of the East; and the cession of Normandy to William Rufus as a pledge for his help in the Crusade. However, William Rufus also came to a sudden end. In the following year, 1100, after a jovial feast he and his companions set out to hunt in the New Forest. In the evening the corpse of the king, with an arrow through the heart, was found by a woodsman. No one has ever known by whom the arrow was sped.

William Rufus was succeeded by his brother, Henry. The new king's chief acts were (1) the granting of a charter of Liberties, (2) his defeat of his brother, Robert, who had attacked him as a claimant of the English throne, (3) the marriage of his daughter Matilda to Geoffrey, Count of Anjou, and (4) the beginning of the establishment of the University of Oxford. Henry's death came suddenly in 1135, while he was in Normandy.

At Henry's death Stephen of Blois, son of the Conqueror's daughter, Adela, was elected king of England. He was at this time forty-one years of age. His reign was characterized by continual warfare, chiefly with Matilda, daughter of Henry I, who was struggling to secure the throne for herself. The civil war continued from 1138 to 1153, with varying turns, until finally it was agreed that Stephen should occupy the throne until his death, at which time it should pass to Matilda's son, Henry of Anjou; to show his good faith Stephen adopted young Henry as his heir. In 1154 Stephen died, and Henry of Anjou became King of England, thus beginning the line of kings known as the Angevins, or Plantagenets.[1] It is this line of kings that is of especial interest to students of Shakespeare's plays, for the ten chronicle plays follow the fortunes of the Plantagenets from King John to Richard III.

When Henry II became king of England he became at the same time the monarch of greatest consequence in Europe. He was king of England; he had feudal rights over Scotland; he was duke of Normandy, count of Anjou and Maine; he was duke of Aquitaine; and he had acquired control over Brittany. This meant, of course, virtual authority over all of France and England. Henry started off doing away with abuses, restoring the Exchequer, and establishing a firm foundation for his strong reign of thirty-five years. He imposed the so-called Great Scutage, instituted the Constitutions of Clarendon, established trial by jury, and formed courts of law. He took part officially in the Third Crusade, though he himself was unable to go. In his reign also there rose to power a churchman named Thomas Becket, who eventually became Henry's Archbishop of Canterbury. Becket for a long time was the man of most consequence in the kingdom, but later he and Henry quarreled, first over the trial of ecclesiastics by civil courts, later over Henry's allowing the Archbishop of York to crown his son King (a ceremony Henry had insisted on in order to insure Richard's future accession), a rite the peculiar privilege of the Archbishop of Canterbury. The result of this last quarrel was the murder of Becket by some of the staunch adherents of the king; the political result was the martyrdom of Becket, whose tomb became the shrine for thousands of pilgrims in later years.

[1] Green, *Short History of the English People*, p. 128, 1875, says: "Geoffrey . . . from his habit of wearing the common broom of Anjou in his helmet had acquired, in addition to his surname of 'The Handsome', the more famous title of 'Plantagenet' ". From French *plante a genet*, broom plant.

In 1189 Henry II, sick and tired, found his French provinces invaded by a French army. He went to defend his property, but he was not now equal to the task. He was forced to capitulate, and died three days later of a fever that had been aggravated by defeat. Founder of the House of Plantagenet, which occupied the throne of England for three hundred and thirty-one years, Henry was one of England's really great kings. He had many gifts, both of mind and body; like all of his ancestors of Anjou, he was thoroughly versed in war, and had the Angevin talent for diplomacy, law, and order. He was vigorous, never idle; his days were spent in war or the chase, in the conduct of business, or in vigorous discussion. These traits combined to produce in Henry II one of England's most able rulers.

On the death of Henry, Richard was immediately accepted as king. The personality of Richard the Lion Heart has secured permanent fame; wherever romance and chivalry are loved the name of Coeur de Lion will be remembered. But his personal share in the administration of English affairs was slight and unimportant. Richard had the power of attracting the personal love of his intimate friends; he was a born adventurer, and his deeds form the foundation of many a medieval story and legend. He was born in 1157; he married Berengaria of Navarre in 1191; he became king of England in 1189. His expedition to the Holy Land, his captivity by Leopold, duke of Austria, on his return from the East, his discovery by his favorite minstrel, his subsequent ransom for the stupendous sum of £100,000, his tournaments, his death by an enemy arrow in his neck as he was laying siege to a castle in France,—all are familiar stories to the average lover of romance. Richard of the Lion Heart died in 1199, ten years after he came to the throne, and John his brother reigned in his stead.

From the Norman Conquest to the accession of John there elapsed one hundred and thirty-three years. In this period six kings sat on the throne of England. Of these six, only two failed to make war on France at one time or another; William Rufus, for the reason that he was for the greater part of his reign defending himself from the attack of his brother Robert of Normandy, and Stephen, because he was kept busy at home defending himself from the determined attacks of Matilda, who was trying to take the English throne for herself. William the Conqueror during the whole of his reign was engaged in more or less open hostility with Philip, king of France; in 1073 an English army attacked Maine; in 1079 William fought with Philip, who had been giving his support to William's rebellious son; in 1087 William again attacked France, and in this expedition he lost his life by accident. In 1106 Henry I invaded France to resist the hostility of Robert, his brother, duke of Normandy. In 1174 Henry II made an expedition into France to put down a rebellion of the barons. And Richard I spent the last years of his life in a constant struggle with Philip Augustus, who represented the natural tendency of the French kings to encroach on the territory of their vassals. In France the Norman dukes were naturally vassals of the French throne; it made no difference to the king of the French that the Norman duke happened to be also king of England. The result therefore was constant vigilance on the part of the English kings to protect their French holdings from the encroachments of the French kings, and an equally constant desire on the part of the rulers of France to wrest from those Normans some part of their rich domains for themselves. It is very interesting to note that this same condition maintained until the time of Henry VI, and forms the plot of several of Shakespeare's plays; for this reason it is important to have an understanding background of Anglo-French relations.

CHAPTER III

King John, 1199-1216

Born 1167. Married 1189, Avice of Gloucester; 1200, Isabella of Angoulême; King of France, Philip Augustus 1180-1223; Pope, Innocent III 1198-1216.

Upon Richard's death the question of his successor naturally arose; in the early days of his reign Richard had regarded Arthur, son of his next oldest brother, as his heir. But later he changed his mind and during his last years he looked upon John as his successor, and on his death-bed he caused his adherents to swear to receive his brother as their king. But Philip of France still favored the cause of young Arthur, and at the death of Richard he made a determined effort to promote Arthur's accession to the crown of England. Aiding Arthur also was his mother, Constance, who was supported by the Bretons. On John's side, however, was Eleanor, his mother, now seventy years old, but still full of energy. The English, preferring the uncle of full age to the immature nephew, elected John king, and he was crowned at Westminster in May, 1199.

In June of the same year John was back in France with an army. He found Philip, pressed by domestic troubles, in a mood to offer favorable terms. John was recognized as lawful ruler of all of Richard's dominions; as a pledge of friendship Louis, Philip's oldest son, was married to Blanche, daughter of Eleanor and Alphonso of Navarre, king of Castile. Because Philip was at that time under an interdict of the Pope, the marriage was solemnized at Rouen.

John then began to make a series of blunders that led to far-reaching consequences. The first act was to divorce his wife, Avice of Gloucester, whom he had married in 1189; this caused the whole family of Gloucester, at all times powerful, to turn against him. His next act was to marry Isabella of Angoulème, fiancée of Hugh, nephew of the powerful Guy of Lusignan. At this the family of Lusignan were enraged, even though the marriage was apparently agreeable to Isabella. In 1202 the Lusignans appealed to Philip, who immediately sponsored their cause, and summoning Arthur to assist him, invaded Normandy, while Arthur laid siege to his grandmother in her castle in France. John went to Eleanor's assistance and by a surprise attack captured Arthur and imprisoned him at Rouen. Later he committed perhaps the greatest of his blunders in having Arthur murdered, though how or when it was done is not certainly known. Matters then began to turn for the worse, and John one by one lost his provinces to Philip until finally by 1204 nothing but the Channel Islands remained to the English king of the hereditary territories of William the Conqueror and Geoffrey of Anjou.

Then came John's trouble with the Pope. In 1205 Hubert Walter, archbishop of Canterbury, died and the necessity arose of securing a successor to him. It had been the custom since the days of William the Conqueror for the ecclesiastics to elect the archbishop, subject to the approval of the king, and this custom had obtained without interference by the king since the days of Becket. But on Hubert's death, the junior ecclesiastics plotted to elect Reginald, a man of no prominence or ability, to the archbishopric, and to get the Pope's approval without that of John, knowing that they could never get John to agree to the plan. John, however, learned of the plot, and forestalled it by insisting on the appointment of John deGrey, one of his officials, a man of great military and administrative ability. The Pope highhandedly refused to approve both of these candidates and persuaded the monks to elect Stephen Langton, an Englishman of great learning and undoubted integrity, but not excessively sympathetic toward King John. Langton had been rector of the University of Paris and had been raised to the Cardinalate by Pope Innocent.

John, however, because of the Pope's highhandedness, refused to admit Stephen Langton into England. In 1208, the Pope in retaliation placed England under an interdict. John was indifferent to Papal interdicts and proceeded to seize the property of all the priests who obeyed the order; the next step was the Pope's. He, in 1209, excommunicated John himself. John's reply was to seize all the property of the bishops. The Pope then issued a threat that he would take immediate steps to have John deposed. This ordinarily would not have affected John in the least, but already there had arisen throughout England so much disaffection and discontent that a distinct movement was seen looking toward John's expulsion. This movement had for one of its manifestations a prophecy by one Peter the Hermit that John would cease to be king within a year.

Philip went on collecting his forces and likewise John lost no time in raising an army to defend himself. John, however, was rapidly becoming very unpopular; the church was against him; the nobles had been so often outraged by the king's inordinate extravagance and his demands upon them that they were against him; and the people were against him. So John, seeking an escape, decided to make peace with the Pope, and agreed to hold England as a fief of the Papacy, to swear fealty to the Pope, and to pay an annual tax to Innocent of one thousand marks. The Pope, after this abject surrender, ordered Philip to desist from his plans against John. But this display of cowardice did not help matters with the king at home.

John again made war on Philip in 1214 and on this expedition John was thoroughly defeated at Bouvines; he was forced to make a peace with Philip and to return to England. Once there, he found the barons demanding the rights given them by Henry I, which John in his stupidity had come completely to ignore. He did everything in his power to put them off, even going so far as to appeal for aid to the Pope. But no help was forthcoming. The barons prepared for war, marched on London, and John received them at Runnymede, near Windsor, on June 15, 1215; he was forced to grant their demands. Thus the Magna Charta was born.

John, however, wanted revenge. He ravaged still further the estates of the barons; the latter in disgust, at the close of 1215, offered the crown of England to Louis, husband of Blanche, and Louis accepted the offer. It remained for him to come and take it. He invaded England, aided by the barons, and John's position looked hopeless. He struggled on, however, won some successes, and finally on his way into Lincolnshire across the sands of the Wash, crossing the channel of the Welland, his baggage was lost in a whirlpool; John, despairing, defeated, prostrate with vexation, made his way to the Abbey of Swinstead. A fever developed there, and he died on October 19, 1216. His death most surely saved him from losing his throne and coming as it did it most certainly saved the kingdom for his descendants. Just what would have happened to the crown of England had John lived six months longer we can only surmise.

The fact remains, however, that his death brought to a close the worst reign in the annals of English history. There is no doubt that John was the worst king ever to sit on the throne in London. Utterly without conscience, absolutely indifferent to right and wrong, fatuously given over entirely to his own desires, he lacked every distinguishing trait of a king; he almost succeeded in ruining England, and did succeed in losing for her all her possessions on French soil. Some of these were won again by later rulers, subsequently to be lost by another weaker but better king; but if John had lived longer it is very probable that he would have lost England itself. Fortunately fate took a hand in national affairs and the nation was saved from utter bankruptcy by his death.

King John
The Play

Historic Time: 1199-1216
Dramatic Time: 7 days
Place: England and France
Purpose: The Effect of a Weak King's Usurpation
Date of Composition: 1593

In no other play has Shakespeare taken so many liberties with history as in *King John*. Examples are many. For instance, the life of the Austrian Archduke who had treated Richard so harshly is prolonged five or six years beyond its actual period for no other purpose than that in the play Richard's natural son may have the honor of avenging his father's wrongs. Too, Richard fell in a quarrel with Vidomar, Viscount of Limoges, one of his own vassals, in 1199, when Leopold of Austria had been dead several years. Shakespeare makes Austria and Limoges one and the same person. Again, Shakespeare pictures the people of Angiers refusing to take either side until the question shall have been decided in battle between the two contestants, whereas history records the fact that Anjou, Touraine, and Maine declared for Arthur from the first, and at no time wavered in their allegiance. Shakespeare represents Arthur as falling from the walls of a castle in England, when as a matter of history he was imprisoned first at Falaise and later at Rouen, where he died. Shakespeare has Constance bewailing the captivity of her son and the ruin of his hopes, when as a matter of fact she died in 1201, the year before Arthur was captured by John. These and many other variations may easily be observed by only a casual comparison of the play with historical fact; but there are two very patent explanations of this difference. In the first place, Shakespeare seized upon the material of history as a source of his plot only so much as was necessary for the dramatic effect he wished to produce; he had to choose the details he needed for the seven days of dramatic action which comprise the play, and naturally a number of incidents had to be combined in order to bring into the action all the details he desired. In the second place, it is now evident that Shakespeare used as the source of his play an older play, written by an unknown author, the plot of which Shakespeare followed very exactly, rewriting the lines of the older play, but not rewriting the story. Thus the historical deviations may easily be understood.

Shakespeare's play of *King John* is based on an earlier play entitled *The Troublesome Raigne of John King of England*, printed for the first time in 1591. This source play was based on Holinshed's *Chronicles*. Shakespeare followed more closely than his wont the plot of this old drama. The creation of the character of Faulconbridge, the episode at Angiers, the marriage of Louis and Blanche, John's dispute with the Pope, John's capture of Arthur, Arthur's death in England, Louis's invasion of England, and John's death are events of the old play blindly followed by Shakespeare; thus Shakespeare is not so much to blame for the unusual warping of history for which he is blamed. We may blame him still, but we at least recognize the source of the trouble.

However, there is a distinct difference in treatment between the two plays. The original play was written when the enthusiasm of the nation was high because of the victory over the Spanish Armada, when the Pope was hurling invective against Queen Elizabeth. It is full of satire and must have been very acceptable to the English people who were now just beginning to realize a great national spirit. An intense hatred of the Papacy runs through both parts of the older play. But Shakespeare in his revision is not so intense against the Pope, save when patriotism demands such an attitude. And it is probable that Shakespeare realized that any radical change in his plot from that of its predecessor would militate against the success of his own play; for that reason he stuck very closely to the events set forth in the work which he copied. Shakespeare almost completely rewrote the dialogue of the older play; there are only two or three unimportant lines that are common to both productions. The older play had no hero, no character to bind the scenes together, thus making an interesting whole. Shakespeare develops the character of Faulconbridge to the extent that he becomes the one outstanding leading personage in the drama, gave him the end-speech of every act but one, and made of him the epitome of those virtues that every Englishman must wish himself to possess.

Shakespeare's *King John* opens with the coming of Philips's ambassador, Chatillon, bringing Philip's ultimatum to John concerning the claim of Arthur to the throne, and with the introduction into the action of Faulconbridge. John, backed by his mother, Eleanor, starts off well, and defies France:

> Be thou as lightning in the eyes of France;
> For ere thou canst report I will be there,
> The thunder of my cannon shall be heard.
> So hence! Be thou the trumpet of our wrath
> And sullen presage of your own decay.
> An honorable conduct let him have.
> Pembroke, look to it. Farewell, Chatillon.

Immediately the king is presented with a dispute to settle, which ends by its settling itself. Robert Faulconbridge and his half-brother, Philip, appear and an argument as to origins ensues. The result is that Philip Faulconbridge admits he is no Faulconbridge at all, but the illegitimate son of Richard Coeur de Lion, and is so accepted by the Court, and acknowledged by John.

The scene swiftly changes to France to the City of Angiers. Philip is there with his son, Louis; Arthur is there, supported by his mother, Constance; with them is the Archduke of Austria, ready to receive the taunts of the Bastard. Chatillon scarcely has time to report before John and his forces appear on the scene, and the rival parties begin bickering for the support of the townsmen of Angiers. The city refuses to accept either of the claimants until the truth of their respective claims is proven by force of arms. To them might made right. However, the two kings had just decided that the better way to settle matters for Angiers was for both of them to bombard the town from opposite directions, when one of the citizens of the city, shrewder than the rest, suggested a substitute: that all differences might be settled amicably by a union between the two hostile forces signalized by the marriage of Louis of France with Blanche of England. This way out was eagerly seized upon by both sides, and the war was over for the time, at least. John thereupon magnanimously gave to Louis the provinces of Touraine, Maine, Poictiers, and Anjou, plus thirty thousand marks of English coin. Is it possible that Shakespeare smiled as he depicted this anticlimax to the hoarse barking of the dogs of war, as he recorded the silly absurdity of John's thunderous challenge to France ending in the ridiculous settlement to which he subscribed and the extravagant gesture by which he willed away with the wave of his hand four of England's choice possessions beyond the seas? The poet causes the Bastard to comment on the debacle:

> Mad world! Mad kings! mad composition!
> John, to stop Arthur's title in the whole,
> Hath willingly departed with a part;
> And France, whose armour conscience buckled on,
> Whom zeal and charity brought to the field
> As God's own soldier, rounded in the ear
> With that same purpose-changer, that sly devil,
> That broker that still breaks the pate of faith,
> That daily break vow, he that wins of all,

>Of kings, of beggars, old men, young men, maids,
>. . . . .
>This bawd, this broker, this all-changing word,
>Clapped on the outward eye of fickle France,
>Hath drawn him from his own determined aim,
>From a resolved and honorable war
>To a most base and vile-concluded peace.

And in the first scene of the third act, Constance says:

>Gone to be married! Gone to swear a peace!
>False blood to false blood joined! Gone to be friends!
>Shall Louis have Blanch and Blanch those provinces?

When Philip verifies for her the previous report of Salisbury, she continues:

>What hath this day deserved? What hath it done,
>That it in golden letters should be set
>Among the high tides in the calendar?
>Nay, rather turn this day out of the week,
>This day of shame, oppression, perjury.

At this point Shakespeare introduces Pandulph, the Pope's legate, demanding an explanation of John for his refusing admission into England of the Pope's choice for Archbishop of Canterbury, Stephen Langton. The boastful John again has recourse to bravado as he replies:

>Tell him this tale; and from the mouth of England
>Add thus much more, that no Italian priest
>Shall tithe or toll in our dominions.

The Pope's answer is excommunication, which at first affected John not at all, but before the play was played the English king surrendered in abject humiliation to "This meddling priest", and even yielded England itself into fiefdom to the "Italian priest". But now he sends the Bastard post-haste to England to rob still further the priesthood, a job peculiarly pleasant to the worldly hero:

>Bell, book, and candle shall not drive me back,
>When gold and silver becks me to come on.

John immediately takes steps to compass the death of Arthur. Shakespeare apparently took delight in his characterization of the king as he records the roundabout way in which John unfolded to Hubert his desires. There is no directness here; all the boldness he employed in his answers to Philip and the Pope is absent when he is brought face to face with the task of discussing the death of his young nephew. And when Hubert comes to the doing of his horrible task his heart fails him; Arthur is spared for the present, only to meet his death shortly in a fall from the battlements of the castle; John, once he has ordered Arthur's death, vacillates not so much from any sense of pity as from fear of what will ensue to him from the barons when they discover he had murdered Arthur, and rejoices when Hubert tells him that he did not carry out the order. But Arthur's accidental death is equally ruinous to John, for there is no one who fails to credit John with his death.

Now news comes that the French under Louis are invading England. All manner of evil omens are seen. Prophets are predicting John's early end; Peter the Hermit stakes his life on a gamble that John will occupy his throne no longer than a year. John, distrait, looks about him for some escape from the trouble that has piled up around him; he makes an abject agreement with the Pope; always the Bastard is there, bolstering up John's waning courage:

> Shall a beardless boy,
> A cock-red silken wanton, brave our fields,
> And flesh his spirit in a warlike soil,
> Mocking the air with colors idly spread,
> And find no check? Let us, my liege, to arms.

Louis, informed by Pandulph of John's about-face, refuses to desist, but determines to go on, claiming the throne for himself. The Bastard takes complete charge of the defense, and handles it manfully. Fate takes a turn at events, the reinforcements of the Dauphin are wrecked on Goodwin Sands, his army is repelled by the genius of Faulconbridge, and England is saved. But the king is poisoned by a monk and lies dying at Swinstead Abbey, and young Henry is at hand to take over the reins of government, so poorly held by his evil-starred father. The play closes with a note that must have sounded sweet to the ears of Elizabethan England, a note uttered by the Bastard:

> This England never did, nor never shall,
> Lie at the proud foot of a conqueror,
> But when it first did help to wound itself.
> Now these her princes are come home again,
> Come the three corners of the world in arms,
> And we shall shock them. Nought shall make us rue,
> If England to itself do rest but true.

John, the man, as he is revealed by history, was boastful, conceited, wicked, weak, cowardly, selfish, and cruel. The portrait that Shakespeare drew of the king is exceedingly true. He has John uttering the most bombastic boasts only to cringe in abject humiliation at his failure to make them good. John defies the Pope, making every show of playing the hero, only to crawl on his very hands and knees in surrender when he finds the Pope getting the best of the argument. He is utterly without any sense of morality, and suspects all others of motives as base as his own. He has not the courage even to be daringly wicked, as Richard of Gloucester had; when things are going his way he struts and boasts; when he suffers reverses he curses his ill-fortune, never realizing for a moment that he alone is responsible for all the misfortunes that came upon him. He cares nothing for England's honor, and is ever ready to trade that honor away when such a trade might possibly redound to his advantage. Shakespeare depicts John truly throughout, but never so truly as when he presents the slinking, cowardly king in the two scenes with Hubert. John tries by hints and innuendoes to make Hubert understand what he desires to be done, without ever committing himself to responsibility for the deed itself. So evil a king he was that it is a wonder England did not suffer even more at his hands than she did suffer.

Shakespeare presents Arthur as a very natural, lovable child. The poet takes liberties with the historical character of Arthur, for the boy was born in 1187 and at the time of his death, April 3, 1203, was sixteen years old. It was twelve years after the death of Arthur that the barons actually offered the crown to Louis. However, for dramatic purposes Shakespeare wished to have Arthur a mere child, and so he became. The boy in the play is artless, gentle, witty, and eloquent. Of the scene with Hubert, Hazlitt has said: "If anything ever were penned, heart-piercing, mixing the extremes of terror and pity, of that which shocks and that which soothes the mind, it is this scene." Of all the children in Shakespeare's dramas, the character of young Arthur is most powerfully and charmingly drawn.

Constance, too, is a finely drawn character. Shakespeare extended her life longer than historical fact justified, but he did so with excellent reason. Actually she died in 1201, two years before her son, but the poet for his dramatic purposes needed her grief over the loss of her child, and this grief is one of the striking qualities of the play. She returns epithet for epithet when Eleanor upbraids her, she rails against the marriage of Louis and Blanche with vehement eloquence, and though she passes from the play in the third act, ere that time she has won the sympathy of all by the beauty of her grief over the loss of Arthur. No artist has ever portrayed better a mother's sorrow than the last words of Constance in the play:

> And, Father Cardinal, I have heard you say
> That we shall see and know our friends in heaven.
> If that be true, I shall see my boy again;
> For since the birth of Cain, the first male child,
> To him that did but yesterday suspire,
> There was not such a gracious creature born.
> But now will canker sorrow eat my bud
> And chase the native beauty from his cheek,
> And he will look as hollow as a ghost,
> As dim and meagre as an ague's fit,
> And so he'll die; and, rising so again,
> When I shall meet him in the court of heaven
> I shall not know him; therefore never, never
> Must I behold my pretty Arthur more.

When the Cardinal attempts to dissuade her from her sorrow, she continues:

> Grief fills the room up of my absent child,
> Lies in his bed, walks up and down with me,
> Puts on his pretty looks, repeats his words,
> Remembers me of all his gracious parts,

> Stuffs out his vacant garments with his form;
> Then, have I reason to be fond of grief?
> Fare you well! Had you such a loss as I,
> I could give better comfort than you do.
> I will not keep this form upon my head,
> When there is such disorder in my wit.
> O Lord! my boy, my Arthur, my fair son!
> My life, my joy, my food, my all the world!
> My widow-comfort, and my sorrow's cure!

But the unifying character of the drama is Faulconbridge. Least historical of all the people in the play, the Bastard seems to represent a composite picture of the typical breezy Briton of his day. He has the irrepressible vigor of animal spirits, a devil-may-care attitude toward life, a manly and courageous heart, a biting tongue, and a broad-minded sense of values that contribute to make him more of a type than an individual. He actually romps through the scenes of the play. He recognizes the baseness of the king, but he treats John with the respect that John's office ought to demand from loyal subjects. When John dies of poison in Swinstead Abbey it is the Bastard who most laments, but even then he recognizes that England needs him and he is ready to respond:

> Art thou gone so? I do but stay behind
> To do the office for thee of revenge,
> And then my soul shall wait on thee to heaven,
> As it on earth hath been thy servant still.
> Now, now, you stars that move in your right spheres,
> Where be your powers? Show now your mended faiths,
> And instantly return with me again,
> To push destruction and perpetual shame
> Out of the weak door of our fainting land.

He hates glib piety, and takes especial relish in despoiling the bishops. By nature he is plain, frank, out-spoken, thoroughly patriotic, loyal, honest, and shrewd to see what is the best course for England's honor. And he, unlike John, is ready to fight to the death for England when her honor is at stake. The typical Englishman, he is what every Englishman might wish to be.

From King John to Richard II,
1216-1377

THE KINGS OF ENGLAND 1272–1399

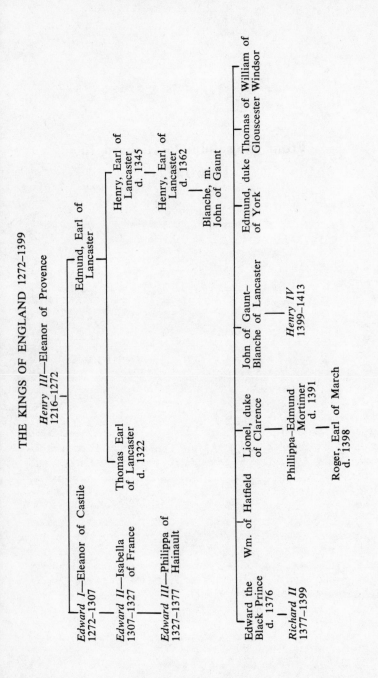

CHAPTER IV

From King John to Richard II, 1216-1377

Henry, John's son, was nine years old when he came to the throne of England as Henry III. The reaction against Louis of France was rapid after John's death, and Henry was crowned on October 28, 1216. Louis was soon forced to retire from England. Affairs of the kingdom during young Henry's minority were entrusted to two able statesmen, The Earl of Pembroke and Hubert de Burgh; Hubert's regime lasted from 1219 to 1232, a regime that succeeded in restoring England to at least a measure of its former peace and power. In 1227, Henry, twenty years old, took over the reins of government, but Hubert's influence was still dominant in the early years of the young King's rule.

Events took their course, and more and more Henry found himself incapable of coping with the forces that were arising around him. Controversies with the Pope continued, and these brought on the rise of the friars, a force that soon was to make itself felt throughout England. Henry grew more and more in debt, until toward 1255 the country was in a state of near-bankruptcy. The barons again decided to assert themselves, this time under the leadership of Simon de Montford, earl of Leicester, who in 1238 had married Eleanor, sister of King Henry. This marriage of one not of royal blood into the royal family caused quite a stir in the royal council, and created a bit of bad feeling. Simon, however, grew gradually into power, and in 1258, when Henry was desperately in debt, when the Mad Parliament met in London, Henry was compelled to yield to the barons, and a council was chosen of twenty-four men, half from the royal council and half from the barons, to enforce all needful reforms. Out of the events growing from this committee's work came the summoning of the famous parliament of 1265, in which may be seen the germ of the first House of Commons. Simon de Montford was the leader in this reform in legislation, and to him goes the credit of initiating the idea of the two Houses of Parliament. This parliament of 1265 was the one outstanding event in the reign of Henry III.

Upon Henry's death in 1272, Edward, his son, assumed the throne at the age of thirty-three years. Few kings had had such an excellent training for the throne as he, for he had spent most of his life in managing affairs of the kingdom, in the barons' war, in Wales, on the Continent, and at home. He chose able ministers and trusted them afterwards. Like most of the kings of this period Edward I had his troubles with France, but he was equal to the situation and no great stir was made on account of it. His reign was particularly note-worthy for the progress he made in legislation, with such steps as the Statute of Mortmain and the Statutes of West-minister. He conquered and reorganized Wales, acted as um-pire in civil strife in Scotland, and organized for himself an army of great strength. In 1295 Edward called the famous Model Parliament, in which were represented the three estates of the realm, the clergy, the nobility, and the commonalty. Trouble with Scotland continued, headed by Wallace and Bruce, and Edward finally overcame the Scots; but somehow it seemed never to do any good to overcome the Scots, for they always had the knack of coming back again, stronger than ever. However, Wallace was captured and executed on London Bridge, and for a while there was peace. Nearly seventy years old now, and worn by an exceedingly strenuous life, Edward found his strength gone. The effort of subduing Bruce, who still was carrying on a guerilla warfare in the wilds of Scot-land, was too great for the old king; he died from over-exer-tion on July 7, 1307.

Edward's was a long reign extending through thirty-five years of struggle at home and abroad; but his reign is con-sidered one of the greatest in English history, in point of leadership, statesmanship, and progress. He resembled Henry

II very closely in the wisdom, strength of character, and generosity of spirit that marked the man, and in the skill with which he always met and handled difficult situations. Edward I was one of England's great rulers.

Edward II, who succeeded his father at the age of twenty-three, was the antithesis of all that characterised Edward I. The young king grew up utterly frivolous and unprincipled; he was selfish and, like John, indifferent to the welfare of the state. His chief weakness was his addiction to favorites, a trait that Christopher Marlowe makes the pivot of his play, *Edward II*, the first great English Chronicle play, one on which Shakespeare modeled most of his own plays concerning this period. The favorite at this time was Piers Gaveston, a Gascon, who had been the king's playfellow as a boy and who now had obtained such influence over young Edward that he seemed incapable of existing happily without Gaveston's presence. The barons resented the preferring of the rank outsider, and they finally forced Edward to dismiss the favorite, a dismissal that was of very short duration, for the king soon found he could not be happy without him and recalled him. This roused the barons to further efforts and again they forced Edward to get rid of Gaveston, which Edward did by giving him important missions among neighboring states. But always he summoned him home. The outcome was that a group of the barons finally reached the point that they could endure Gaveston no longer, and he was captured and executed, an act that came near to breaking Edward's heart.

Edward II inherited Robert Bruce from his father without receiving his father's ability to cope with him, with the result that success after success marked Bruce's efforts to stir up trouble in Scotland. Matters came to a head in the battle of Bannockburn in 1314. The English were defeated and the work of Scottish independence was complete.

Edward's penchant for favorites again flared up, this time in the case of the Hugh Despensers, father and son, who so flagrantly presumed on the power of their influence with the king as to disgust the whole of the nobility. Other troubles arose. In 1325 Isabella, the Queen, went to France on official business, and while there she formed a liaison with Roger Mortimer, a disgruntled baron. Together they formed a plot against the king of England and the favorites. The result was that Edward was forced to flee from England, but finally fell into the hands of his enemies. Mortimer assumed charge of affairs in England, and the Despensers were executed. Edward II was forced to abdicate the throne in favor of his son; he was given into the custody of one of his bitter enemies and was murdered in Berkeley Castle September 21, 1327. Mortimer and Isabella soon discovered that young Edward, now king, intended to be king in fact; Isabella was deprived of all her wealth and was kept by her son a prisoner in the manor of Rising until her death in 1358; Mortimer was promptly hanged.

Edward III was born in 1312, and was fifteen years of age at the time he was made king. His was a long reign, lasting through fifty years, during which time Charles IV, Philip VI, John, and Charles V were kings in France. Edward was above all things else a soldier; his code was the code of chivalry; scrupulously courteous, he was little affected by the laws of Christian moralty; he was a knight to the core, but withal he was vain, selfish, and pitiless. He regarded England as only a source for men and money with which to carry on his wars, with the result that he increased his country's prestige abroad but caused great dissatisfaction at home.

Edward's first military efforts were directed against Scotland, where he supported the claim of Edward Balliol to the Scottish throne. Out of this war came the French wars that occupied Edward for so long a time. The Scottish patriots had formed an alliance with the king of France; to punish France Edward decided to invade that country, and his first move was to lay claim to the crown of France upon the death of Charles IV in 1328. The claim was far-fetched,[2] but it served

2   PHILIP III d. 1285

| Philip IV | | | | |
| d. 1314 | | | Charles of Valois | |

| Louis X | Philip V | Charles IV | Isabella m. | Philip of Valois |
| d. 1316 | d. 1322 | d. 1328 | Edward II | |

John	Joan		Edward III	
d. 1316	Charles the			
	Bad			

as an excellent excuse for an invasion. In 1316 died John I, the infant son of Louis X, who had succeeded his father, Philip the Fair, in 1314, and himself died in the following year. Anxious to avoid giving the crown to Louis's daughter Joan, then a mere child, the French nobles invoked an old law of the Franks called The Salic Law, which disqualified a woman from reigning, and gave the throne to Louis's next brother, Philip V. In 1322 he too died, leaving only daughters, and the precedent having been established, the crown passed to his brother Charles IV. At his death without a son in 1328, (since his sister Isabella was married to a foreign king) the crown passed to Charles's cousin, Philip of Valois. So now Edward III of England made claim to the French throne through his mother Isabella, though the French themselves had invoked the Salic law to prevent women with more claim than Isabella from becoming rulers of France.

Edward continued his efforts against France, and in 1346 he crossed the Channel into Normandy with his armies. He found contact with the French army at Crécy on August 26, and after a fierce battle the English were victorious. The credit for the victory has been given to the prince of Wales, called the Black Prince, because of the great skill in leadership he displayed at Crécy. Edward next laid siege to Calais, and the city was forced to capitulate. This brought to an end the campaign in France; aside from the glory of the victory, this war with France brought Edward little good. He failed to acquire the crown of France by his efforts; indeed it is doubtful if he actually expected success in that direction.

But a great tragedy overtook England in 1349. The Black Death, coming from China by infectious stages along the trade routes, reached Constantinople in 1347, came to Italy in 1348, and was brought into England early in 1349. It is hard to know how many persons in England died of this terrible disease before it finally died out, because there were no registers of births and deaths in those days, and in the distraught state of affairs caused by the terror of the plague no records were kept; but modern calculation puts the mortality in England at one death in every three persons in the kingdom. The high and the low, the rich and the poor fell before the grim disease; Edward's daughter was among the victims.

In 1356 Edward again invaded France in the person of his oldest son, the Black Prince. The French met the English forces at Poitiers on September 19, and the result was a complete rout of the French; the French king, John, with his son was captured, and France was for the first time at the mercy of the English. The result was the so-called Great Peace of Bretigny, signed in 1360; by this treaty Edward gave up his claim to the French crown and to Normandy, Anjou, and Maine; but he was to keep in full sovereignty all of Aquitaine, Ponthieu, and Calais. In addition the French were to pay a large ransom for the restoration of their king—a sum too large for impoverished France, and John languished in London in prison until he died, unransomed, in 1364.

Then the English began to suffer reverses. The Spaniards defeated the English fleet at Rochelle; an expedition into France under John of Gaunt was disastrous; the Black Prince secured a very dubious victory later by the massacre of Limoges, where in a fit of temper he ordered every man, woman, and child of the city to be put to death. With all the warfare made by Edward on France in his long reign, with the two great English successes of Crécy and Poitiers, with the complete debacle of France in 1360, it seems as if some profit might have accrued to England; but from a distant perspective it appears that so far as England was concerned all the energy, all the expense, all the hardship, were in vain. England owned as little territory on the Continent at the close of Edward's reign as she possessed at the beginning, with the single exception of Calais. But to Edward war was meat and drink, and it mattered little to him that England had to foot the bill. Edward died in June, 1377, and was succeeded by his grandson, Richard, son of the Black Prince. Here Shakespeare again takes up the thread of the story.

CHAPTER V

Richard II, 1377-1399

Born 1366; married, 1381, Anne of Bohemia; 1395, Isabella of France. King of France: Charles V., d. 1380; Charles VI., d. 1422.

Edward III died in 1377; the Black Prince, his son, had died in June, 1376. Thus the succession passed by the law of primogeniture to the son of the Black Prince, Richard. He was only eleven years of age, and his accession is a strong proof of the popularity of his father and of the strength of the idea of hereditary right, for, with the exception of Edward III, hitherto no minor, who had an uncle of full age ready to take the crown, had been allowed to accede to the throne. During Richard's minority, as in the case of Edward III, a Council was appointed to handle the affairs of the kingdom until the young king should be able to take over the government himself. To avoid jealousy the uncles of the king were not included in this Council, and the young king was left in the guardianship of his mother, Joan of Kent, widow of the Black Prince.

The greatest event of the early years of Richard II was the Peasant's Revolt of 1381. The actuating cause of this revolt was the poll-tax of 1381, though there were a number of subsidiary reasons. The exchequer was so low and the need for money so great that parliament in 1379 had levied a poll-tax, graduated so that dukes paid six pounds, thirteen shillings, four pence, earls paid four pounds, and so on down to the villein in the country. The amount fell short of what was needed and in 1380 another poll-tax was levied, and the graduation of this was not so fair; thus it was brought home to everyone the consequences of ill-government and extravagance. In June, 1381, there was an uprising of Kentishmen under Wat Tyler and John Ball; everywhere in the southeast manors were burnt and tax rolls destroyed; every lawyer on whom the peasants could lay hands was put to death; led by Wat Tyler the Kentishmen crossed the Thames at London Bridge, murdered the Archbishop of Canterbury, and threatened the city. Richard met the revolters face to face and boldly won them over by his promises and persuaded them to go home. Wat Tyler was stabbed by the mayor of London. Parliament met and refused to sanction the promises made by Richard; thus the peasants seemed to have lost their cause entirely.

The second important movement that confronted Richard was the rising power of the Lollards, followers of John Wyclif. Wyclif had his stronghold at Oxford University, where he went on popularizing his ideas and organizing poor priests who were to go through the land preaching his doctrines. Then he also completed a translation of the Bible into English, an act that gave his reputation a very firm foundation. But his movement met resistance from the bishop of London, who succeeded in driving Wyclif and his followers from Oxford. But there was no law for the burning of heretics in England, so Wyclif was personally unharmed. His tenets spread fast, and the saying was that "if you saw five men talking together, three were Wyclifites." Richard's queen, Anne of Bohemia, herself became a convert of Wyclif.

A third problem confronted young Richard. The young king was addicted to favorites, like his great-grandfather Edward II; the difference being that Richard chose for his favorites members of his own court, and at times they were so numerous and influential that they may be called the Court Party. Against these men, however, a powerful opposition was being organized by Thomas of Gloucester, the king's uncle, and by Henry of Bolingbroke, the king's cousin, son of John of Gaunt. This opposition grew so strong that eventually Richard was forced to do away with his system of favorites, and yield to the demands of the nobles. Richard ruled very ably for a while, and the country enjoyed peace and prosperity; literature came into its own in the persons of Wyclif, Chaucer, and Langland; but Richard's chief fault seems to have been his idleness, and eventually this led to his deterioration. In 1394 his wife, Anne of

Bohemia, died, and removed thereby the excellent influence of her peace-loving nature from the affairs of the nation. The same year the wife of John of Gaunt died, Constance of Castile, and he immediately married the nurse of his children, Katherine Swynford, by whom he already had a number of children. To oblige his uncle, Richard promoted an act of parliament legitimizing the children of Katherine Swynford, and the Beauforts, as they were called, took their place in history— an important place as it later proved to be. In 1396 Richard went to Paris and married Isabella, a child at that time of eight years, daughter of Charles VI of France. While in Paris Richard's head seems to have been turned by the splendor and luxury of the French Court, and he resolved to return to England and institute the same regal splendor in London. From that time dates his decline.

Richard then undertook a sudden move against the barons who were all the time harassing him. In July 1397 he suddenly arrested Gloucester, Arundel, and Warwick; he called parliament to meet at Westminister, at which time he completely overawed it with an array of 4,000 archers with arrows aimed if parliament failed to do his behests. Richard then formed a royalist party in the Commons led by Sir John Bushy, Sir Thomas Green, and Sir William Bagot; he induced parliament to accuse Gloucester, Arundel, and Warwick of treason; they performed nobly, with the result that Arundel was beheaded immediately, Gloucester was sent to Calais under guard and was there murdered, and Warwick was exiled to the Isle of Man for his life.

Then a quarrel arose between Bolingbroke and Norfolk. In December 1397 the new dukes of Hereford and Norfolk were riding between Brentford and London when, so Bolingbroke reported, Norfolk informed him that Richard intended to put to death both Henry Bolingbroke and his father, John of Gaunt. When Richard heard of this he summoned them before parliament where the two gave each other the lie and quarreled fiercely. Richard referred the matter to a court of chivalry, which ordered the two to decide the affair by combat in the lists at Coventry on September 16, 1398. But when the two entered the field ready for the joust Richard stopped the fight and ordered Norfolk into exile for life and Hereford for ten years, a span he later remitted to seven. The manifest injustice of this judgment was great; it is apparent that the king took this means of getting two troublesome lords out of the kingdom, and at the same time he assured himself that Bolingbroke in exile would not tell too many tales concerning the royal responsibility for the death of Gloucester.

But John of Gaunt died in February, 1399. With Gaunt dead and his son, Henry, exiled, the king took occasion to seize the property of the Lancasters in order to raise money to equip an expedition into Ireland, an act he had promised Henry he would not do. Richard sailed to Ireland in May, 1399, leaving his uncle York in charge of the throne. Henry Bolingbroke, receiving news of this state of affairs, on pretence of coming to protect his property, landed in Yorkshire on the 4th of July, and demanded the restoration of his family estates. Henry was immediately joined by Percy, Earl of Northumberland, who himself had a personal grievance against Richard, and by many another baron. Henry's arrival was the signal for a general uprising against the king; all the friends of Gloucester, all who felt they had been injured by Richard's tyranny, all who thought they had had enough of the unscrupulousness of the king who thought he could do no wrong, gathered under Bolingbroke's banners. On July 27, even York joined with Hereford. Richard, returning from Ireland, met Henry at Flint Castle, went with him to London, where just before parliament met on the 30th of September he signed his name to a document that ended his reign for all time: he absolved his subjects from all fealty and allegiance; he renounced every claim to the throne; declared himself insufficient and useless; and stated that he desired his successor to be Henry Bolingbroke, Earl of Hereford, Duke of Lancaster. This document was read to parliament which in turn prepared a statement giving thirty-three reasons why Richard should be deposed; the interesting fact about this statement is that none of the reasons given was trivial. Parliament then declared Richard deposed.

Henry of Lancaster claimed the crown as his by right of descent from Edward III by right of conquest; he was accepted and became king in one of the strangest bloodless revolutions of all times. Richard was ordered by the new government to be removed to some safe place and there to be kept, and that he should have no communication of any kind whatsoever with anyone. He was taken to Leeds Castle, in Kent, and later to Pontefract Castle. A rebellion was organized by some who were still friends of Richard, including the earls of Huntingdon, Kent, Rutland, and Salisbury; at a critical moment, however, Rutland revealed the plot to his father, York, who lost no time in informing Henry. The plot was soon past history. And to prevent any such future occurrences, Henry decided it were best to have Richard entirely out of the way, where his friends would not be tempted again to help him; therefore Richard was put to death at Pontefract. By January, 1400, it was generally accepted that he was dead; a body said to be his was publicly exhibited and buried, and for some time no one doubted that his death was a fact. Yet no one historically has ever known the exact date or manner of his end, and two years later rumors spread that he had escaped and was still alive. However, they never materialized into anything more solid than mere rumors, and historians believe that Henry had him quietly murdered in Pontefract.

King Richard II
The Play

Historic Time: 1398-1400
Dramatic Time: 14 Days
Place: England
Purpose: Legitimacy vs. Aptitude
Date of Composition: 1595

The Tragedy of King Richard II was written by Shakespeare in the year 1595. Shakespeare drew the materials for this, as for most others of his English history plays, from the *Chronicle* of Holinshed. The historic time of the play extends from February, 1398, to March 1400. In this play are found no such great wanderings from historical fact as occurred in *King John*; and again whatever divergence exists is due to the exigencies of dramatic necessity. Holinshed is followed very closely throughout. The play, however, is highly unified and concentrated, differing from the rambling, epic type represented in the three parts of *Henry VI*, which cover a period embracing the whole of the reign of Henry VI. In *Richard II* the dramatist has chosen two years of dramatic action and presented it compactly and concisely. In some places he has brought historical events more closely together than they were actually in history, in order to insure more compactness of action. Yet the play gives a fair impression of the rule of King Richard, despite the fact that the dramatist uses only two years from a reign of twenty-two.

The theme of the play is *Legitimacy* vs. *Aptitude*. It is a two-man play, differing from *Richard III* in that respect, and showing that Shakespeare is getting away from the influence of Marlowe, whose four one-man plays are the greatest of pre-Shakespearean dramas. England had never been a country that blandly accepted any or every claimant to the crown simply on grounds of heredity; heredity played a strong part, of course, but for a long time the power of the people to express themselves had been growing, and when a legitimate heir to the throne proved himself unworthy the people were ready to displace him and welcome a substitute. The people too were becoming tired of experimenting with child kings, though it took them a long time to learn their lesson. Their experience with Henry VI, for instance, did not prevent their going ahead and accepting the young son of Edward IV; but the willingness they exhibited toward Edward V's deposition and their acceptance of Richard of Gloucester proves that they had had about enough of minority rule. So here we have pictured the weakness and shortsightedness of Richard contrasted to the strength and ability of Bolingbroke. Shakespeare is careful to see that the reader has sufficient sympathy for the trembling Richard, but he also takes care that the actions of Henry shall be approved by the public who see or read his play.

The play opens with the King holding court in his palace in London, having summoned Bolingbroke and Mowbray to appear to present their sides of the quarrel in which they have recently come to blows. All the pageantry of feudalism is there; Richard, accompanied by his nobles, sits in judgment; he is supreme. This scene is the outcome of a superiority complex the king built up while he was in France, having beheld the autocracy and splendor of the French king; he decided that he would conduct himself in England on a scale commensurable with that of Charles VI. Bolingbroke and Mowbray appear, and toss back and forth various and sundry charges against each other; Bolingbroke accuses Mowbray, the Duke of Norfolk, with being the instigator of all the treason that has existed for eighteen years in England; he adds that Mowbray was responsible for the death of the Duke of Gloucester in Calais. Mowbray explains himself, and challenges Bolingbroke to fight. The king then utters judgment: let the quarrel be settled in fair fight in the jousts at Coventry on a set day, and the scene is over. So far Richard has command of the situation.

The day set for the trial in the lists comes. Richard is there with his court; the contestants appear, girded for the battle. The king stops them before they engage, and decided to settle the affair to suit himself. Norfolk he banished for life; Bolingbroke is exiled for ten years, which later at the plea of John of Gaunt, Henry's father, the king commutes to six. There follows some of the best poetry in the play—the farewell instructions of Gaunt to his son, somewhat reminiscent of Polonius's advice to Laertes as the boy was starting out to Paris to attend school. Gaunt says:

> All places that the eye of heaven visits
> Are to a wise man ports and happy havens.
> Teach thy necessity to reason thus;
> There is no virtue like necessity.
> Think not the King did banish thee,
> But thou the King. Woe doth the heavier sit
> Where it perceives it is but faintly borne.
> Go, say I sent thee forth to purchase honor
> And not the King exiled thee; or suppose
> Devouring pestilence hangs in our air
> And thou art flying to a fresher clime.
> Look, what thy soul holds dear, imagine it
> To lie that way thou goest, not whence thou comest.
> Suppose the singing birds musicians,
> The grass whereon thou tread'st the presence strewed,
> The flowers fair ladies, and thy steps no more
> Than a delightful measure or a dance;
> For gnarling sorrow hath less power to bite
> The man that mocks at it and sets it light.

But to the banished Bolingbroke this advice seems hard to follow, for he says, "Who can hold a fire in his hand by thinking on the frosty Caucasus?" Imagination plays small part in the career of Bolingbroke; he is not one to accept buffets calmly, and seek no redress. And the first act closes with a scene that reveals Richard's real reason in this removing from the kingdom a man who he had already discovered was dangerous.

Then we come to the death of Gaunt. The old Duke is lying sick, attended by his brother York. We see already York's attitude toward Richard, preparing us for his going over to Bolingbroke's side later in the play. York thinks Richard will not deign to visit Gaunt as he is about to die. But Gaunt says:

> O, but they say the tongues of dying men
> Enforce attention like deep harmony.
> Where words are scarce, they are seldom spent in vain,
> For they breathe truth that breathe their words in pain.
> He that no more must say is listened more
> Than they whom youth and ease have taught to glose.
> More are men's ends marked than their lives before.
> The setting sun, and music at the close,
> As the last taste of sweets, is sweetest last,
> Writ in remembrance more than things long past.

Old Gaunt then breaks forth in that long panegyric of England's greatness comprising lines 40-58 of Act II, Scene I, a passage that was extracted and printed in a collection of similar poems of patriotism published at that time, called *England's Helicon*. But at the end he adds that all this "dear, dear land" is now leased out by the insufficiency of a very poor king. And soon, when the king does come, together with his favorites and his wife, Gaunt continues to speak his mind concerning the evil condition of the kingdom to a degree that Richard's anger is kindled savagely; he calls his uncle "a lunatic lean-witted fool" and tells him that his kinship alone saves him from being beheaded then and there. But Gaunt is not daunted, and goes so far as to accuse Richard of his brother Gloucester's death. And a little later Gaunt's death is announced by Northumberland, when he tells the king that Gaunt's tongue is now a stringless instrument."

Shakespeare's portrait of Gaunt is entirely unhistorical. He was born at Ghent (hence his surname) in 1340, and in 1398 he was the eldest surviving son of Edward III. Neither abroad nor at home had his career been glorious, nor had he shown any of the remarkable patriotic tendencies and emotions which have been attributed to him in the play. The great victories of the early campaigns belonged to the Black Prince and the king, and Gaunt's contribution had been a disastrous campaign in Spain and an equally disastrous expedition into France in 1373-5. The result of his efforts was almost the complete loss of Edward's gains in France. Historically, his abilities were fair, but his personal character was bad, and he had little skill in winning popularity. He never acquired any real hold over the people at large, and his chief influence was exerted as a leader of the nobility. Shakespeare takes a self-seeking, turbulent, and far from patriotic politician and exalts him into an embodiment of the love of country in its noblest form. But the dramatic character of old John of Gaunt, "time-honoured Lancaster" is splendidly drawn, and he forms one of the main personages in the play.

Immediately upon Gaunt's death Richard fatuously decides to seize for himself all the properties of the Lancasters, against the advice of the Duke of York. Richard sets out for Ireland; the Queen has presentiments of impending misfortune. Bolingbroke lands at Ravenspurgh, and the nobles flock to his standard. The Duke of York, who had been left as regent in England during the king's absence, decides to join with Henry. Richard returns tardily from Ireland, and realizes the condition of his affairs. True to his nature, at one time he is overbearing, autocratic; at another he becomes morose, downcast, in despair. At one time he says:

> Not all the water in the rough rude sea
> Can wash the balm off from an anointed king;
> The breath of worldly men cannot depose
> The deputy elected by the Lord.

Then almost immediately a reaction sets in and he loses his self-confidence; he becomes melancholy; he philosophises:

> Of comfort no man speak.
> Let's talk of graves, of worms, and epitaphs;
> Make dust our paper and with rainy eyes
> Write sorrow on the bosom of the earth.
> Let's choose executors and talk of wills;
> And yet not so; for what can we bequeath
> Save our deposed bodies to the ground?

Richard and Bolingbroke meet, and Bolingbroke courteously but firmly handles the situation. The contrast between the two men is never more clearly brought out than in these scenes. Henry deposes Richard, takes the crown for himself, causes Richard to sign a paper admitting his own guilt, and Richard is sent into custody to Pomfret Castle. Shakespeare causes Richard to have one more fling at manhood; when Exton and the servants come to murder him, the deposed king seizes an axe and lays about him savagely, killing two of the servants; he is then himself struck down by Exton. In this account Shakespeare followed closely the narrative of Holinshed, who describes thus Richard's end:

"Sir Piers of Exton entred the chamber, well armed, with eight tall men likewise armed, euerie of them having a bill in his hand. King Richard, perceiving this, put the table from him, &, steping to the formost man, wrung the bill out of his hands, & so valiantlie defended himselfe, that he slue foure of those that thus came to assaile him. Sir Piers, being half dismaied herewith, lept into the chere where king Richard was wont to sit, while the other foure persons fought with him, and chased him about the chamber. And in conclusion, as king Richard trauersed his ground, from one side of the chamber to the other, & coming by the chere, where sir Piers stood, he was felled with a stroke of a pollax which sir Piers gaue him vpon the head, and therewith rid him out of life; without giuing him respit once to call to God for mercie of his passed offenses."

But Henry, now king, when he is told by Exton of the accomplishing of the murder, is smitten in conscience for this thing of which he is so guilty. Exton gets no reward from Henry, but is sent out into banishment for having done what he had been told to do. And the king sadly finds that conscience is a powerful thing; he wishes vainly that he might undo his evil, but finds that impossible. The next best thing, therefore, is to expiate his guilt by penance, and he promises that in his reign he will wash off the blood of his cousin from his guilty hand by making a trip to the Holy Land. All through his troublesome reign this deed worked on his conscience, and when he too came to die he had one regret, that he had never succeeded in removing from his soul the guilt of the murder of his cousin, Richard II.

The second scene of Act V is interesting in that it presents two striking episodes: the description of the entry into London and the discovery of Aumerle's plot. The description of the entry into the city is wholly imaginary, for Richard's conveyance to the Tower and Bolingbroke's entry into London did not occur on the same day. But the dramatic effect of the contrast between the two kings, one deposed and one usurping, is very great; the portrait of Richard acquiring something of the distinction of persecution meekly borne contrasted with the portrait of the victorious and triumphant Bolingbroke is finely drawn. Described by the Duke of York for the benefit of his wife, the contrast between the two main characters of the play is exceedingly effective. Then, following immediately upon this comes the detecting of young Aumerle in his plot against Henry; Shakespeare again departs from historical accuracy in making The Duchess of York mother of Aumerle; she was actually his stepmother. Aumerle's mother, the first duchess, had died in 1394. The duchess of the play was York's second wife, Joan Holland, third daughter of Thomas, Earl of Kent, son of Joan Plantagenet who afterwards became the wife of the Black Prince and mother of Richard II. The duchess was therefore actually Richard's niece by birth and his aunt by marriage. It is doubtful if Shakespeare knew of this relationship nor of the age of the young duchess.

Isabella of France, daughter of Charles VI, was born in 1388, and married Richard II in 1396; at the time of the play she was just ten years old. As a child of ten years she could scarcely be of much consequence dramatically, so the dramatist proceeded to transform her into a mature woman for his dramatic effect. He uses her to bring home to us by her devotion something of Richard's personal charm. As a matter of fact, towards the end of the play only two persons remained faithful to the deposed king: his wife and his former groom. Isabel grieves to see Richard in so sad a plight as he passes her in the street leading to the Tower. Throughout all of his troubles she has been with him in spirit; she sees him taken from her:

> But soft, but see, or rather do not see,
> My fair rose wither; yet look up, behold,
> That you in pity may dissolve to dew,
> And wash him fresh again with true-love tears.

And the conversation of the two which ends with his going to the Tower and her being sent back to France is as full of pathos as may be found anywhere in Shakespeare. The love introduced here is used merely to enhance the pathos of the political catastrophe; even to Isabella he is a changed man, but her devotion is unchanged. And we feel that Shakespeare has done well to create the character of the Queen as he has done.

Then finally we find a link that connects this play with the one that is to follow. These connecting links are always interesting, showing that Shakespeare, though he did not compose the historical plays in chronological order, nevertheless had in mind the whole plan of the series as he wrote. In the third scene of Act V we have Henry asking:

> Can no man tell me of my unthrifty son?
> Tis full three months since I did see him last.
> If any plague hang over us, 'tis he.
> I would to God, my lords, he might be found.
> Inquire at London, 'mongst the taverns there,
> For there, they say, he daily doth frequent,
> With unrestrained loose companions,
> Even such, they say, as stand in narrow lanes,
> And beat our watch, and rob our passengers;

And when Percy reports that he had seen the young prince at Oxford lately and that Hal had said he was going to "go unto the stews and from the commonest creature pluck a glove, and wear it as a favor" in a joust, Henry replied:

> As dissolute as desperate; yet through both
> I see some sparks of better hope, which elder years
> May happily bring forth.

Young Hal was at this time exactly twelve years old. Our first introduction to him was in character with the portrait drawn of him in the two succeeding plays; and Shakespeare wishes us to realize early that all the boy's escapades in the taverns of London were merely training for his destiny as England's Ideal King.

CHAPTER VI

Henry IV, 1399-1413

Born 1366; married 1380 Mary de Bohun; 1403 Joan of Navarre. King of France, Charles VI, d. 1422

Among the kings of England the name of Henry IV should rank very high, both in point of personal ability and strength of character, but, sandwiched between Richard II and Henry V as he was, historians have somewhat lost sight of the performance of Bolingbroke because of the pity incited for his predecessor and the brilliant achievements of his son. The early days of Henry's reign were occupied with consolidating his position on the throne and protecting himself from conspiracies and rebellions that were constantly being formed against him. No sooner had he succeeded in suppressing the rebellion in favor of Richard than he found himself compelled to invade Scotland in an effort to suppress the perennial rebellion there. The uprising there had developed to large proportions, led by a man named Glendower, who possessed a genius for the sort of warfare as was carried on in the mountainous regions on the border of Wales. When Henry invaded Wales in September, 1400, Glendower retired into the mountain fastnesses, and Henry was compelled to withdraw, leaving his young son Henry, thirteen years old, to guard the border, under the tutelage of Henry Percy, son of the Earl of Northumberland. The conduct of the Scottish war was left to the Earl of Northumberland; in 1402 Edmund Mortimer, at the head of a body of Englishmen defeated the Scots at Nesbit Moor, while Henry Percy defeated a large Scotch army at Holmedon Hill. But reverses followed Henry IV, for Glendower succeeded always in defeating the

English and finally captured Mortimer, who had attacked him. Henry began to become unpopular, and his finances came to a very low ebb.

It was in this state of affairs that the Percies—Northumberland and his son Hotspur—decided to start an insurrection against Henry. It is true that Northumberland had aided Henry in the overthrow of Richard, but that was due to discontent against Richard and not to any love the old earl might have had for Bolingbroke. And now Henry was in debt to the Percies for a large sum of money, and the king had failed to accomplish anything against Glendower. The impending quarrel came to a head in Henry's demanding the surrender of the prisoners taken at Holmedon Hill, and the Percies' refusal to turn them over, unless the king should pay them what he owed them. In addition to this, Henry refused to pay ransom to Glendower for the return of Edmund Mortimer, whom he had captured, and since Mortimer's sister, Elizabeth, was Hotspur's wife, it became a family affair. Henry's chief reason for not paying the ransom was the fact that Mortimer was a possible claimant for the crown, and the king was glad to have him out of the way, held prisoner by Owen Glendower. Mortimer's captivity, however, was not so hardly borne, for it turned out that Mortimer married the daughter of Glendower, and an alliance was formed between Glendower and the Percies, the result of which was the flaring up of another rebellion against the king.

When Henry received news of this uprising he immediately marched against the rebels and met them at Shrewsbury on July 21, 1403. The result of the battle was a complete victory for the king's forces, though the struggle was one of the most severe in English history. Henry Percy (Hotspur) fell in the battle, and several of the leaders were captured. Hotspur's head was exposed on London Bridge for a month as a warning to all those who should thereafter choose to take arms against the power of the king. After Hotspur's death the rebellion soon disintegrated, though Owen Glendower at no time ever capitulated; when Henry died Glendower was still there, darting in and out of his mountain retreats to make raids on the border. His pertinacity served at least one purpose: from 1407 onward the warfare against Glendower was conducted by young Henry, Prince of Wales, who acquired on the Welsh borders the military

experience which afterwards served him so well when he became king.

Henry had next to deal with a conspiracy in which the old
Earl of Northumberland figured, which included Thomas Mowbray, Earl of Nottingham, son of the late Duke of Norfolk, and
Richard Scrope, Archbishop of York. An expedition was organized with 8000 men and moved against the king; they were
met near York by an army under the king's third son, John,
later the Duke of Bedford, and after certain negotiations the
army dispersed, but Mowbray and Scrope were arrested and
immediately beheaded. The public execution of a churchman
aroused universal horror in England, and the affair appeared
for a while to assume the proportions of a martyrdom. But apparently rebellion was for the present at an end.

However, Henry's throne had been no sinecure. The prolonged struggle with Glendower and the Scots, the warfare with
the Percies, the financial troubles at home, and the realization
that he had gained the throne by force and must keep it by
might had combined to make the crown taken from Richard II
not so desirable a thing as he had at first imagined. No one
without the strength of character and iron determination of
Henry Bolingbroke would have struggled through the difficulties
of his reign. These struggles did have the effect of leaving
Henry at the end of his first eight years of royalty an enfeebled
and weary man; and though the last six years were quiet and
peaceful, yet they were spent by the king in a losing battle with
disease; he became a hopeless invalid, and his son, Prince Henry,
assumed a large part of the responsibility of the realm while
the king was incapacitated. Henry IV grew worse as the months
passed, and died in March, 1413. Shakespeare paints him as
a king whose conscience forever hurt him for his illegal usurping
of Richard's throne and murder of Richard, an act the expiation
of which had been Henry's purpose continually since his accession. It seems that he considered the only method whereby he
might wash himself clean of the guilt of Richard's death was
a pilgrimage to the Holy Land; a visit to Jerusalem would purge
him of his guilt. But he had so many troubles at home that he
never attempted a crusade, and Shakespeare pictures his disap-
pointment at his failures, when dying he causes the old king to
find some consolation at least that the chamber in which he

is lying is called the "Jerusalem Chamber"; that was as near as he ever got to Jerusalem. Holinshed gives thus his version:

> "At length, he recouered his speech, and, understanding and perceiuing himselfe in a straunge place which he knew not, he willed to know if the chamber had anie particular name; wherevnto answer was made, that it was called Ierusalem. Then said the king: "Lauds be giuen to the father of heaven, for now I know that I shall die heere in this chamber; according to the prophesie of me declared, that I should depart this life in Ierusalem."

Whatever may be said of Henry Bolingbroke, it is an evident fact that he made an honest effort to govern constitutionally, to be a parliamentary sovereign. That fact is perhaps the outstanding quality of his reign. He chose members of parliament to be his continuous council; the control of parliament over finance was complete; regular sessions of the House of Commons were summoned; the Speaker of the House of Commons was made the spokesman of all reports on finance. The strict adherence to constitutional principles in his relations to the two houses of Parliament makes Henry's reign extremely noteworthy among the early kings of England, and this fact indicates the honesty of purpose that prompted Henry in all his dealings with his various governmental agencies. His name should be greater among the rulers of England. It would be greater, perhaps, if he had not had so brilliant a son.

Henry IV, Part I.
The Play

Historic Time: September 14, 1402-July 21, 1403
Dramatic Time: 10 days
Place: England and Wales
Purpose: To idealize Prince Hal
Date of Composition: 1597

The date of composition of this play is 1597. It was first published in quarto form in 1598, and entered in the Stationers' Registers under date of February 25, 1598; a second quarto edition was brought out in 1599, and others in 1604, 1608, and 1613. It was mentioned by Meres in his list in 1598.

Shakespeare drew the material for this play, like that of all of the historical plays, from Holinshed's *Chronicles*. In addition, there was an old play entitled *The Famous Victories of Henry the Fifth,* from which the dramatist probably derived some material, particularly concerning Falstaff, for in the old play a Sir John Oldcastle appears as one of Prince Hal's wild companions, and it is apparent that Shakespeare introduced him as a character in his play, later changing the name to Sir John Falstaff in order not wantonly to offend the Protestant party. In the first quarto edition of *Henry IV, Part 2* there is found the prefix *"Old."* before one of the speeches of Falstaff; in the first act Henry calls the knight "my old lad of the castle"; and in the third act Falstaff is said to be "page to Thomas Mowbray, Duke of Norfolk," an office Oldcastle actually held. From the old play mentioned above, the author and date of which are uncertain, Shakespeare also derived material for his later play, *Henry V.*

The action opens with the king still harping on his intention of making a crusade to the Holy Land in an effort to expiate his guilt of having displaced and murdered his predecessor, Richard. He had given orders that plans be made for such an expedition. But just as he is receiving a report on these plans news comes of disaster to an English force under Mortimer leading an expedition against the unruly Glendower in Wales. Upon the heels of this bad news is the report of Hotspur's successes at Holmedon, which causes the king to have mingled feelings: joy at the success of his forces and envy that Hotspur should be the man so successful. For from this point starts the contrast between Henry Percy, otherwise known as Hotspur, and Hal, Prince of Wales. The king thus expresses his emotions:

> O that it could be proved
> that some night-tripping fairy had exchanged
> In cradle-clothes our children where they lay,
> And call'd mine Percy, his Plantagenet!

Hotspur refuses to turn over to the king the prisoners he has taken at Holmedon, an action that starts a quarrel between the two that soon grows to great proportions. The crusade is indefinitely postponed and King Henry gets down to business at home. The Percies, Northumberland and his son, and Worcester, enter into a conspiracy to unite with Glendower against the king. Glendower is willing and we see the rebellion getting under way. One of the best scenes of the play is the first scene of Act III, where we see Hotspur, Glendower, and Mortimer dividing the map among them, territory as yet unconquered, but which they have every hope of taking. Hotspur's character is well delineated here:

> Methinks my moiety, north from Burton here,
> In quantity equals not one of yours.
> See how this river comes me cranking in
> And cuts me from the best of all my land
> A huge half-moon, a monstrous cantle out.
> I'll have the current in this place damm'd up;
> And here the smug and silver Trent shall run
> In a new channel, fair and evenly.
> It shall not run with such a deep indent,
> To rob me of so rich a bottom here.

And when Glendower objects to any such procedure, Hotspur says nothing can stop him from doing it. He tells Glendower when the latter tells him he cannot do it, he had better speak it in Welsh, a language Hotspur cannot understand. Then, when Glendower amiably agrees that he may turn the Trent, Hotspur declines, saying he will give thrice so much land to any well deserving friend, but when it comes to making bargains he will cavil "on the ninth part of a hair."

The scene continues with Mortimer and his wife, who is Glendower's daughter and a Welsh lady, whose language Mortimer cannot understand at all, trying to communicate with each other, the results of which conversation are rather meager.

Back in London the king has summoned the Prince of Wales from his taverns in order to converse with him on more serious topics. The upbraidings of the king impress young Hal and he convinces his father that he is ready to act his part in the coming suppression of the rebellion. Hal realizes that his honor is at stake, that he is to be pitted against the romantic Hotspur, and he resolves to acquit himself well. Report comes of the gathering of the rebels at Shrewsbury, and a plan of campaign is laid out by the king.

The rival forces array themselves at Shrewsbury. After a
number of skirmishes Hotspur faces Hal on the field of battle,
a meeting that has been planned for by the dramatist throughout
the entire play. Hal has to prove himself by his conduct with
Hotspur, who represents the flower of all that is noble and chi-
valrous and romantic. Only one outcome is possible, of course.
Hal overcomes Hotspur, and wins for himself the renown which
in the eyes of the dramatist proves the young prince's manhood.

And here takes place the action of another of the really great
scenes of the play. While Hotspur and Hal are engaged, Falstaff wanders on the scene, but Douglas also approaches and
engages Falstaff, who falls and pretends that he is dead. After
Hal has slain Hotspur, he turns and spies Falstaff lying dead,
and utters over his body his sincere regret at the untimely end
of his old friend. When Hal has gone, Falstaff gets up, throws
the body of Hotspur on his back, after having again pierced
him with his own sword, and wobbles into the presence of Hal
and his brother John. He reports that he has had a terrific
struggle with Hotspur after Hal had left, that Hotspur had not
been killed at first, but only stunned, that he had recovered and
that he, Falstaff, had fought him fiercely a long hour "by Shrewsbury clock", and had finally despatched him. The prince, good
sport that he is, does not give him away.

The play ends with the close of the battle of Shrewsbury,
and we see the king starting off to fight with Glendower still
further, while young John is delegated to go to put down the
uprising of Scrope and Northumberland. We are given a final
glimpse of the sportsmanship of young Hal as he gives freedom to one of his captives who had that day so well acquitted
himself in battle, the Earl Douglas. Falstaff lives to continue
his pleasantries in another play.

The main point of the play, of course, is the action that
turns about the characters of Hotspur and young Hal. Shakespeare wished to eulogise young Henry to the utmost degree,
and to do so he spared no pains to embellish the character of
Hotspur to its fullest extent, thereby transferring all the manly
qualities of Hotspur finally to Hal, who conquered him. To do
so Shakespeare was forced to take liberties with historical fact,
for in order to pit the two against each other he necessarily had
to make them of nearly the same age. Actually Hotspur was

some twenty years older than Hal, having been born in 1366; and Hal actually served under Hotspur in the campaigns on the Welsh and Scottish borders, but historically he at no time ever came in hostile contact with him. Shakespeare wields a lavish brush when he undertakes to paint Hotspur for us. The Prince was accurate in his description of him:

> He that kills me some six or seven dozen of Scots
> at a breakfast, washes his hands, and says to his wife,
> "Fie upon this quiet life! I want work." "O my sweet
> Harry," says she, "how many hast thou killed today?"
> "Give my roan horse a drench," says he: and answers
> "Some fourteen," an hour after; "a trifle, a trifle."

Equally good is the third scene of Act II. Hotspur is introduced reading a letter from George Dunbar, Earl of March, in Scotland. His soliloquy is wonderfully revealing of character. Lady Percy comes in, and wonders why he has acted so strangely of late. When she inquires of him the cause, he answers by calling "What, ho!" to a servant. The servant enters, carries on quite a conversation with his master, retires, and then Hotspur says, "What say'st thou, my lady?" Enough to make any lady mad. And he makes matters worse by telling her:

> This evening I must leave you, gentle Kate.
> I know you wise; but yet no farther wise
> Than Harry Percy's wife. Constant you are,
> But yet a woman; and for secrecy,
> No lady closer; for I well believe
> Thou wilt not utter what thou dost not know;
> And so far will I trust thee, gentle Kate.

One can easily see in this talk of his that he really does love her, and she knows it. We see her again, in the next play, reproaching Northumberland because he had not gone to the assistance of her Hotspur when he needed him, and again she lets us know her deep affection for the rough soldierly husband whose bark was worse than his bite. Her name was not Kate, by the way, but Elizabeth. She was Lady Elizabeth Mortimer, sister to Edmund, the Lord Mortimer of this play. Shakespeare may have mistaken her name, or he may have changed it to Kate because of a seeming fondness for that name that he manifested on many occasions.

There is many another excellent brushstroke in Shakespeare's picture of Hotspur. When we first see him we observe his disgust at the mincing, perfumed young lord who had come from the king to demand his prisoners. And his contempt for his wife's mild oaths:

> In good sooth!
> Heart, you swear like a comfit-maker's wife.
> "Not you, in good sooth," and "as true as I live,"
> and "as God shall mend me," and "as sure as day;"
> Swear me, Kate, like a lady as thou art,
> A good mouth-filling oath, and leave "in sooth"
> To velvet-guards and Sunday citizens.

Nor does Hotspur, the soldier, care for such gentle things as music. When his wife cautions him to lie still and listen to the Welsh lady sing, he replies, "I had rather hear Lady, my brach, howl in Irish."

But one of the really deft touches in the portrait of Hotspur occurs in the next play, when Kate is reproaching her father-in-law for his tardiness as the cause of her husband's death. He did not go to the wars when his going would save her husband, and now she thought it utterly useless for him to go. She continues:

> There were two honors lost, yours and your son's.
> For yours, the God of heaven brighten it.
> For his, it stuck upon him as the sun
> In the grey vault of heaven, and by his light
> Did all the chivalry of England move
> To do brave acts. He was indeed the glass
> Wherein the noble youth did dress themselves.
> He had no legs that practised not his gait;
> And speaking thick, which nature made his blemish
> Became the accents of the valiant;
> For those that could speak low and tardily
> Would turn their own perfection to abuse
> To seem like him; so that in speech, in gait,
> In diet, in affections of delight,
> In military rules, humours of blood,

> He was the mark and glass, copy and book,
> That fashioned others.

The magical touches by which Shakespeare created the imperishable likenesses of his historical characters are no better shown than in his inimitable portrayal of Glendower, the Welsh warrior who was so long the thorn in the side of Henry the king. Glendower spelt his full name thus: Owain ap Gruffydd, lord of Glyn-dyfrdwy, which means the Valley of the Black Water or Dee. Westmoreland in the first scene of the play calls him "the irregular and wild Glendower"; Holinshed relates that when the king pursued him into the mountains, Owen "conveyed himself out of the way into his known lurking-places and, as was thought, through art magic he caused such foul weather of winds, tempest, rain, snow, and hail to be raised for the annoyance of the king's army that the like had not been heard of." Glendower himself reports that at his nativity

> The front of heaven was full of fiery shapes,
> Of burning cressets; and at my birth
> The frame and huge foundation of the earth
> Shaked like a coward.

Though Hotspur laughed at what he considered these idle boastings of huge Glendower, the warrior insisted that his was a no ordinary beginning. Hotspur has no patience with all the witchcraft that Glendower claims, and says that:

> Sometime he angers me
> With telling me of the moldwarp and the ant,
> Of the dreamer Merlin and his prophecies,
> And of a dragon and a finless fish,
> A clip-wing'd griffin and a moulten raven,
> A couching lion and a ramping cat,
> And such a deal of skimble-skamble stuff
> As puts me from my faith. I tell you what:
> He held me last night at least nine hours
> In reckoning up the several devils' names
> That were his lackeys.

Glendower was in reality a remarkable man; he was well educated, had been a law student at Westminster and had been

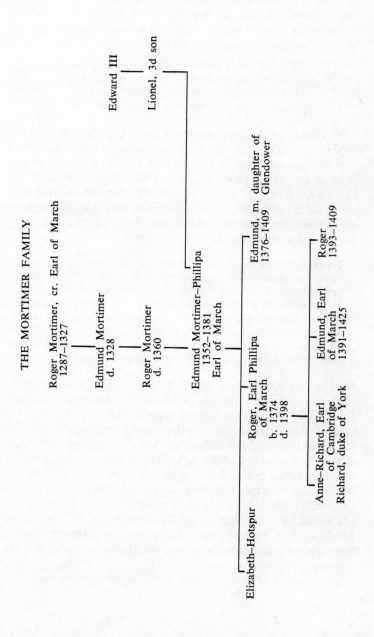

THE MORTIMER FAMILY

Edward III
Lionel, 3d son

Roger Mortimer, cr. Earl of March
1287–1327

Edmund Mortimer
d. 1328

Roger Mortimer
d. 1360

Edmund Mortimer–Phillipa
1352–1381
Earl of March

Edmund, m. daughter of
1376–1409   Glendower

Roger, Earl   Phillipa
of March
b. 1374
d. 1398

Elizabeth–Hotspur

Anne–Richard, Earl
of Cambridge
Richard, duke of York

Edmund, Earl
of March
1391–1425

Roger
1393–1409

an esquire of Henry himself before he came to the throne. He was polished, elegant, talented, cultured, artistic, but withal a genius in the border warfare that he knew so well to wage. His boast in the play is very true when he says:

> Three times hath Henry Bolingbroke made head
> Against my power; thrice from the banks of Wye,
> And sandy-bottomed Severn, have I sent him
> Bootless home, and weather-beaten back.

Mortimer, in the play, has been for a long time a source of confusion to critics of the historical plays; some critics think that Shakespeare made a mistake in his man, and point to passages in the play to prove the point; others think that the chroniclers who form the source of material themselves were mistaken in his personality. In some respects both bodies of opinion are correct. For instance, Holinshed, from whom Shakespeare got his material chiefly, says:

> The king began not a little to muse at this request (that Mortimer be ransomed), and not without cause: for indeed it touched him somewhat neere, sith this Edmund was sonne to Roger earle of March, sonne to the ladie Philip, daughter of Lionell duke of Clarence, the third sonne of king Edward the third; which Edmund, at king Richards going into Ireland, was proclaimed heire apparent to the crowne and and realme; whose aunt, called Elianor, the lord Henrie Persie had married.

Shakespeare, in *I Henry IV*, Act I, scene II, speaks of Hotspur's demanding the ransom of Mortimer, "his brother-in-law". Here, too, the poet calls him the Earl of March. But in Act III, scene I, Mortimer in conversation with Glendower concerning the ladies says, "Good father, tell her she and my *aunt* Percy shall follow in your conduct speedily." It does appear, as Hudson and other critics have suggested, that here Shakespeare mistook Sir Edmund Mortimer for his nephew, young Edmund, his brother, the Earl of March. But again, in Act II, scene III, line 80 he has Lady Percy speaking of Mortimer as "my brother Mortimer." If Shakespeare did confuse the Mortimers, uncle and nephew, the blame may rest on Holinshed, who did the same.

As a matter of fact, a glance at the accompanying table will show exactly who Mortimer in the play was. He was the youngest son of Edmund Mortimer, third Earl of March, and Philippa, daughter of Lionel, Duke of Clarence, and heiress of Ulster. He was born at Ludlow November 9, 1376. On the death of his older brother, Roger, in 1398, Edmund became by reason of the minority of his nephew the most prominent of the Mortimer connection in Wales. He joined Henry Boling-broke on his way to depose Richard II. He was brother-in-law to Hotspur, and assisted Hotspur against the rebellion of Glendower. On June 22, 1402, he was taken captive by Glendower, who treated him well because of his prominence and because of his connection with the family pretending to the throne of England. The Percies busied themselves about procuring his ransom, but Henry IV felt that he was a potential danger to his own tenure of the throne, and refused to help deliver him from Glendower, thinking him safer in captivity. Henry forbade the Percies to take any steps toward procuring Mortimer's freedom, and on October 19, 1402, made the grievous error of seizing the plate and jewels of Edmund —an action very similar to that of Richard when he confiscated Henry's own property while Henry was in exile. This action turned Mortimer against the king, and after that he made common cause with Glendower. On November 30 of that same year he married Glendower's daughter with great pomp and solemnity. The revolt of the Per-cies followed immediately, in which Glendower and Mortimer joined, the result of which is common knowledge. After 1404 Glendower's cause lost ground, and Mortimer was reduced to great distress. He was finally besieged in Harlech Castle in 1409, and perished during the siege.

As for young Edmund Mortimer, Earl of March, he was at the time the play begins exactly eleven years old. This Edmund was eldest son of Roger, fourth Earl of March, and Eleanor Holland, and was therefore nephew of the Edmund Mortimer of the play. In his seventh year he succeeded to the titles and estates of the Mortimers and became thus the Earl of March. Since Richard II had already recognized his father Roger as heir-presumptive to the throne, the young earl was now re-garded by all of Richard's adherents as their future king; but Richard's fall in 1399 changed that status, and Henry IV took young Edmund and his younger brother Roger (Edmund and

Roger seemed to be favorite names among the Mortimers) and put them under guard at Windsor under pretext that they were the king's wards—a benevolent custody it was, but Henry simply wished to have the two young Mortimers always under his watchful eye, in order that their friends and relatives might not have the opportunity to organize around them a rebellion that might point toward their being placed on the throne. They were continued in this benevolent and kindly guardianship until the king's death in 1413; they were given every privilege except unlimited freedom, and were kept with the king's own children, John and Philippa. On February 13, 1405, a bold attempt was made to carry the young Mortimers off to join Glendower and their uncle in Wales. They actually were gotten away, but were caught and brought back.

When Henry V acceded to the throne he felt himself so securely placed that he released young Edmund and restored him to his estates, his younger brother Roger having died in 1409. The young earl remained faithful to Henry V throughout, although in 1415 Richard, Earl of Cambridge, who was married to Anne, sister of young Mortimer, formed a plot to take him to Wales and to have him proclaimed king there. For this plot Richard lost his head, but no guilt seems to have been imputed to Mortimer, and the young earl continued to hold Henry's friendship and trust. He served in France with Henry, and died January 19, 1425. There being no heir, the Mortimer line thus came to its end and the titles and estates of the Mortimers passed through Anne to her son, Richard of York.

So it seems that Shakespeare must have had in mind some of the events that pertained to young Edmund Mortimer while he had reference to the uncle, Sir Edmund Mortimer; some critics have suggested that to Shakespeare *any* Mortimer would do, so long as he was a Mortimer, and since the poet's knowledge of the facts was somewhat hazy, and his source material did not assist him very much, it was natural that some confusion would result. However, there is not enough fog to cause the average student much concern.

As for Falstaff perhaps there has been as much written concerning him as about any character in all of Shakespeare. Johnson said of him that he was a compound of sense and vice; he has been called thief, glutton, coward, boaster, cheat, bully, and clown; he was fat, coarse, salacious, stupid, gross, and always drunk; but in spite of all of these unpleasant characteristics he was witty, not malicious, a good fellow, and seemed very fond of his companions. The first speech of the Prince in the play describes Falstaff admirably: "Thou art so fat-witted, while drinking of old sack and unbuttoning thee after supper and sleeping upon benches after noon, that thou has forgotten to demand that truly which thou wouldst truly know. What the devil hast thou to do with the time of the day? Unless hours were cups of sack, and minutes capons, and clocks the tongues of bawds, and dials the sign of leaping-houses, and the blessed sun himself a fair hot wench in flamecoloured taffeta, I see no reason why thou shouldst be so superfluous to demand the time of the day." Thus Shakespeare draws Falstaff as clearly and as deftly as he defines all the personages that move across his pages. The Prince recognizes Falstaff and his other companions for what they are, and plays with them with his eyes open, knowing that when it becomes necessary for him to withdraw from them and cast them off, his reformation will be the more remarked.

Falstaff serves several offices in the two plays of *Henry IV*. For one thing, he and his cronies are a means for the education of Hal. Shakespeare would have us think that Hal will be the better king for his having served an apprenticeship among the taverns of Eastcheap. The young prince is among the roisterers of the alleyways but he is never of them. He is all the time learning by contact, getting experience that will serve him in good stead in later years. Hal realizes this, for he says at the beginning:

> I know you all, and will a while uphold
> The unyoked humour of your idleness;
> Yet herein I will imitate the sun,
> Who doth permit the base contagious clouds
> To smother up his beauty from the world,
> That when he please again to be himself
> Being wanted, he may be more wondered at
> By breaking through the foul and ugly mists
> Of vapors that did seem to strangle him.

In the second place, Falstaff forms the pivot for the humor of the play. To some, today, Falstaff's wit may seem to be no wit at all, but it must be remembered that Shakespeare was writing to please the crowd who watched the play from the pit, and he adapted the humour to their wit. What appeared as humour in Shakespeare's day probably would not pass current today. Still, taken by and large, there are humorous situations in the Falstaff motif that are great, especially his fight at Shrewsbury, and the robbery scene. Any audience today would enjoy those escapades. In the third place, the Falstaff part of the play furnishes the poet with a filler, so to speak; he had too much material for one play of five acts, and too little for two plays; by introducing Falstaff and his coterie Shakespeare makes out two full plays of five acts each, which was required of him by the rules of the theater of that time. And finally, Falstaff represents the decline of chivalry. He is the burlesque of a knighthood that was rapidly becoming a thing of the past, decadent and on its last legs. No better than in the character of fat, pompous, cheap Sir John could Shakespeare portray the pass to which knighthood had come as the system of feudalism so firmly established by William the Conqueror was now rapidly approaching its end. It is a far cry from the autocratic pageantry of knighthood pictured in *Richard II* to the pseudo-chivalry represented by Falstaff.

Henry IV, Part II
The Play

Historic Time: July 21, 1403 -April 9, 1413.
Dramatic Time: 9 days.
Place: England.
Purpose: Reformation of Hal
Date of Composition: 1598

The play was first published in quarto form in 1600; it had been entered upon the Stationers' Register on August 23, 1600. Its date of composition is 1598, and it was written immediately after the completion of *Henry IV, Part I*. The play was written prior to the writing of Ben Jonson's *Every Man Out of his Humour,* acted in 1599, for in Jonson's work Justice Silence is mentioned.

Holinshed's *Chronicles* is the source of the material of this play, though Shakespeare took some of the events from the old drama, *The Famous Victories of Henry Fifth.*

We are introduced to the action of the play by the arrival of Lord Bardolph before the castle of Warkworth, where he finds the old Earl of Northumberland, waiting for news of his son's progress. Bardolph informs him that Hotspur is victorious, that the king's forces are defeated and that Prince Henry is killed in action. No sooner had Bardolph completed his erroneous report than one of Northumberland's retainers named Travers arrives with the report that conditions are exactly the reverse of what he had been told, and that Shrewsbury was lost and his son, Hotspur, killed. This report is verified by the arrival of another retainer, Morton. The earl, giving vent to his grief at the death of his son and the defeat of his hopes, decides to join forces with the rebellious Bishop of York, who was then marching against the king. Upon the earnest solicitation of his wife and daughter-in-law, however, he is constrained to postpone entering the contest. In the meantime the conspirator York, together with Mowbray and Hastings, pushes his expedition against the king, and meets the forces of Henry led by young John of Lancaster, son of the king, in Yorkshire in the Forest of Gaultree. John sends Westmoreland to arrange with the rebel leaders terms of a truce looking to a peaceful settlement; the Archbishop agrees to meet Prince John; they arrange the terms for a cessation of hostilities. When the rebels have performed their part of the bargain and have dismissed their troops Prince John then violates his honor by ordering Westmoreland to arrest the rebel leaders and promises them speedy punishment for their treason. The king is told of the happy outcome of these affairs, together with the added news that the Earl of Northumberland has been overthrown by the forces of the Sheriff of Yorkshire; but at the moment Henry hears the tidings that should cause him joy, he is stricken with illness, and realizes that his end is approaching. Prince Henry is summoned; there occurs the scene in which the Prince, coming upon his father very ill, thinks he is dead, and takes the crown from the pillow and puts it upon his own head, an act the sick king, on recovering slightly, misconstrues. After words of counsel to the young prince the king dies. Hal is crowned king. His first act was one of magnanimity to the Chief Justice who had imposed the law on the prince in his wilder days and now expected the new king to take his revenge. Henry Fifth started right. The second sign of royal strength of character was his breaking off entirely with Falstaff, who was expecting great things now his young friend had become king. But Henry sternly rebuked old Sir John when he presented himself, and banished him from his presence forever, to the great delight of his brother John and the Chief Justice. The play ends on a note of prophecy by John predicting renewed war with France, which in Shakespeare's inimitable way links the action of his play with that of its sequel, *Henry V*.

Henry Bolingbroke found that sitting on the throne of England was not at all times the pleasant thing he perhaps had imagined it would be. From the time he assumed the throne he constantly was forced to defend himself from plots to displace him. No sooner had he been crowned than the followers of Richard organized a plan to remove Henry and restore Richard to his former place, a plan that was betrayed by the marplot Aumerle. The presence of the Mortimers in his realm was ever a potential threat against which he at all times had to be on guard. The rebellion of the Percies and the continual guerilla warfare carried on by Owen Glendower made his reign one long struggle. Not till the suppression of the plot of the Archbishop of York (and that was done by trickery) did Henry find himself at liberty to remain quietly unmolested by those who were his enemies, personal or political. And then it was too late for him to enjoy this freedom from attack, for he was the victim of a disease that made him for the latter years of his reign a complete invalid. Henry speaks somewhat of the cares of kinghood in what is perhaps the finest poetical passage in the play when he says:

> How many thousand of my poorest subjects
> Are at this hour asleep! O Sleep, O gentle Sleep,
> Nature's soft nurse, how have I frighted thee,
> That thou no more wilt weigh my eyelids down
> And steep my senses in forgetfulness?
> Why rather, Sleep, liest thou in smoky cribs,
> Upon uneasy pallets stretching thee,
> And hushed with buzzing night flies to thy slumber,
> Than in the perfumed chambers of the great
> Under the canopies of costly state,

And lulled with sound of sweetest melody?
O thou dull god, why liest thou with the vile
In loathsome beds, and leavest the kingly couch
A watch-case or a common 'larum-bell?
Wilt thou upon the high and giddy mast
Seal up the ship-boy's eyes, and rock his brains
In cradle of the rude imperious surge
And in the visitation of the winds,
Who take the ruffian billows by the top,
Curling their monstrous heads and hanging them
With deafening clamor in the slippery clouds,
That, with the hurly, Death itself awakes?
Canst thou, O partial Sleep, give thy repose
To the wet sea-boy in an hour so rude,
And in the calmest and most stillest night
With all appliances and means to boot,
Deny it to a king? Then happy low, lie down!
Uneasy lies the head that wears a crown.

And even the young Prince of Wales, speaking not from experience but from observation, continues the same thought when he says:

Why doth the crown lie there upon his pillow
Being so troublesome a bedfellow?
O polished perturbation! golden care!
That keep'st the ports of slumber opened wide
To many a watchful night! Sleep with it now!
Yet not so sound and half so deeply sweet
As he whose brow with homely biggen bound
Snores out the watch of night. O majesty!
When thou dost pinch thy bearer, thou dost sit
Like a rich armor worn in heat of day,
That scald'st with safety.

The king continues his ruminations on the burdens of kingship in his last words of advice to his son, Henry:

God knows, my son,
By what by-paths and indirect crook'd ways
I met this crown; and I myself know well
How troublesome it sat upon my head.
To thee it shall descend with better quiet,
Better opinion, better confirmation;

> For all the soil of the achievement goes
> With me into the earth. It seem'd in me
> But as an honour snatched with boist'rous hand,
> And I had many living to upbraid
> My gain of it by their assistances;
> Which daily grew to quarrel and to bloodshed,
> Wounding supposed peace. All these bold fears
> Thou see'st with peril peril I have answered;
> For all my reign hath been but as a scene
> Acting that argument; and now my death
> Changes the mode; for what in me was purchased
> Falls upon thee in more fairer sort;
> Yet, though thou stand'st more sure than I could do,
> Thou are not firm enough, since griefs are green;
> And all my friends, which thou must make thy friends,
> Have but their stings and teeth newly ta'en out.

The king then gives good advice concerning keeping the peace at home, when he tells Hal:

> Be it thy course to busy giddy minds
> With foreign quarrels, that action, hence borne out,
> May waste the memory of the former days.
> More would I, but my lungs are wasted so
> That strength of speech is utterly denied me.
> How I came by the crown, O God forgive;
> And grant it may with thee in true peace live!

And now a word about that last great scene where the new king meets with Falstaff for the last time. When Sir John learned of the death of the king and the accession of Hal, he immediately made plans to go to him, feeling sure that Hal would make him at least his prime minister. "The laws of England are at my commandment; blessed are they that have been my friends," he says. His great day has come. But the king comes by in royal state, accompanied by the Lord Chief Justice. Falstaff greets him as in the old days with a wink and buffoon words. The young king says, "My Lord Chief Justice, speak to that vain man," and then to Falstaff the king himself speaks:

> I know thee not, old man; fall to thy prayers.
> How ill white hairs become a fool and jester!

I have long dreamed of such a kind of man,
So surfeit-swelled, so old, and so profane;
But being awaked, I do despise my dream.
Make less thy body hence, and more thy grace;
Leave gormandizing; know the grave doth gape
For thee thrice wider than for other men.
Reply not to me with a fool-born jest.
Presume not that I am the thing I was;
For God doth know, so shall the world perceive,
That I have turned away my former self;
So will I those that kept me company.

There is a lot of pathos there, in the crestfallen attitude of the old knight. He turns to Shallow and says, "Master Shallow, I owe you a thousand pounds." But he simply cannot believe that his Hal means what he has said; of course the new king had to act this way in company; but once he is in the privacy of his palace the king will send for him, and all will be well. But Sir John is hustled off to Fleet Prison. However, we are led to believe that Hal was lenient with him, and that he soon released him, for in the next play we hear of Falstaff at liberty, though his heart is broken.

Many have criticized Henry V for his treatment of his old companion of Eastcheap. Many have concluded that Hal was after all a poor sport, that so long as he was merely Prince Hal he consorted with Falstaff and his companions, but once he assumed the royal dignity, it went to his head and he became too proud for further intercourse with them. Nothing of course is farther from the truth. Shakespeare's whole story of Falstaff, from his first appearance in the play on to this scene, led directly to just this denouement; this was perhaps the main reason for Falstaff's being: to show Hal's complete reformation, once he became king. Hard as it may seem to us who enjoy fair play, Henry V could do nothing else with Falstaff than what he did; his action was indicated from the beginning. So the dramatic necessity of the story demanded the harsh treatment of Falstaff. Besides, from the standpoint of etiquette it never would have done to have allowed Henry, the ideal king, to consort further with the tavern rascals. Thus are Shakespeare and Hal vindicated.

One striking fact remains to be mentioned. The two plays of

Heny IV are the only ones of the whole series in which the queen of England has no part. In *King John* Isabella had no part, but Queen Eleanor is there, John's mother. In *Richard II* Isabella, his wife, was advanced from adolescence to maturity in order to function dramatically as the king's wife, supporting him in his troubles. In *Henry V* we see the courtship and marriage of Henry and Katharine. In *Henry VI*, through the three plays Margaret holds one of the leading parts. In *Richard III* a number of queens pass in review: Elizabeth Woodville, Margaret, Anne. But in the *Henry IV* plays there is no queen; there are several ladies present: Lady Percy, Lady Mortimer, and Lady Northumberland; the only mention of the queen, the only suggestion that there was a queen, occurs in Act II, scene IV, lines 320-322 of the First Part, when the Prince, on being told there was a nobleman at the door come to see him, sent by his father, replies, "Give him as much as will make him a royal man, and send him back again to my mother." The mother of Hal was Mary de Bohun, whom his father had married in 1380; she was the youngest of the heiresses of the earldom of Hereford, and her older sister had already married Henry's uncle, Thomas of Woodstock, Duke of Gloucester. Henry the Fifth's mother[3] died June 10, 1394, five years before her husband became king; she therefore never enjoyed the privilege of reigning as queen of England. On February 7, 1403, Henry IV married for the second time, his second wife being Joan of Navarre, widow of John IV, duke of Brittany, daughter of Charles the Bad of Navarre. Just what Shakespeare would have us understand concerning Hal's speech mentioned above is doubtful; he may have had in mind his stepmother, whom his father had just married, or he may have meant nothing further than a play on the words, father and mother, without any further significance.

3   THE SONS OF HENRY IV ARE AS FOLLOWS:

Henry IV–Mary de Bohun

Henry V 1388–1422	Thomas, Duke of Clarence 1389–1421	John, Duke of Bedford 1390–1435	Humphrey, Duke of Gloucester 1391–1447

CHAPTER VII

Henry V, 1413-1422

Born 1388; married, 1420, Katharine of France
King of France, Charles VI, died 1422.

About the name of Henry V there hovers more glamor than about that of any other king of England. All historians agree, it seems, that he was the greatest of England's kings; none before him have been so illustrious, nor have any since his reign approached him in that quality which makes for an ideal king. Shakespeare put forth his best effort to portray him as the epitome of all the virtues a royal character is supposed to possess. He was an able warrior, a great administrator, a man of high and great courage, a gentleman of honor. The story of Henry V is the story of the ideal king.

His first act, on becoming king, was to give the chancellorship to his uncle, Henry Beaufort, Bishop of Winchester. He made the Earl of Arundel his treasurer. He had the remains of Richard II honorably interred at Westminister; he restored the ancestral lands of the Percies to the sons of Hotspur; he made a confidential friend of the young Earl of March; he did all he could do to show that bygones were bygones.

In 1415 Henry was prepared to declare war on France. He chose a favorable moment, for the Burgundians and Armagnacs were quarreling, and Henry hoped that one or the other party would take sides with him. In 1414 he sent a demand to France that the provinces of Normandy, Maine, Anjou, and Gascony be restored to English hands. Naturally, this demand was rejected, and Henry, with Parliament backing him, prepared an invasion of France.

When the troops were ready to embark at Southampton,

a plot against the king was discovered, centering around the young Earl of March. The leader of the plot was Richard, Earl of Cambridge, who had married Anne Mortimer, sister of the Earl of March. Others in the plot were Lord Scrope and Sir Thomas Grey. They had plotted to seize the Earl of March after Henry had departed for France, to carry him to Wales, and there have him crowned king of England, intending to establish his claim to the crown. It is doubtful if young Edmund entered into this plot at all, and some historians say that it was Edmund himself who revealed the plot to Henry. At any rate, the conspiracy was found out, and the conspirators were beheaded. With the conviction, of course, went the loss of the titles held by those guilty. Henry remained in close friendship with March, and he further showed his magnanimity by taking the young son of Cambridge and having him brought up in his own court. This boy was Richard, later Duke of York, the foe of Henry VI.

Landing in France Henry laid siege to the fortress of Harfleur, which he finally took. The king then started toward Calais, but was intercepted at Agincourt by a large French army, which actually outnumbered the English seven to one. On October 25, 1415, Henry gave battle, and in spite of inferior numbers he won a decisive victory. The English immediately marched to Calais, and returned to England.

Brilliant as the success at Agincourt was, it had done little toward a conquest of France which Henry devoutly wished; he immediately set about to organize another invasion of that country, and he did it in a much more thorough manner. In 1417 he again crossed to Harfleur, and spent the years 1417, 1418, and 1419 besieging the French fortresses which were being doggedly defended by the French, who were not risking an engagement in open warfare. In the first part of 1419 he succeeded in capturing Rouen, then Pontoise, and his way into Paris was unopposed. Henry made his demands, which were agreed to by the French at Troyes on May 24, 1420. These terms were: That Henry should marry Katherine, daughter of the French king; that Henry should be regent of France until the death of Charles VI; and that Henry should be king of France upon the death of Charles VI. On June 3, 1420, Henry and Katherine were married. He returned with his bride to

England in February, 1421, having left his brother, the Duke of Clarence, to represent him in Paris.

Henry returned to France in June 1421, to repress the French who had proven too strong for Clarence. He again defeated them. Every battle that Henry ever engaged in he won, though often against great odds; every town that he ever laid siege to he took. But he fell a victim to dysentery, and lost. He died at Vincennes on August 31st, 1422, at the age of thirty-four.

King Henry V
The Play

Historic Time: 1415-1420.
Dramatic Time: 9 days.
Place: England and France.
Purpose: The Glorification of Hal.
Date of Composition: 1599.

The source of the material of this play, like that of all the Chronicles, is Holinshed's *Chronicles*. Shakespeare follows the main thread of the actual events, altering the order only slightly, but condensing the action to suit his needs. The long speeches in the play are Shakespeare's, with the exception of the genealogical argument of Canterbury, which follows Holinshed closely. Practically all the extra-historical material in the play is original with the poet, including the excellent characters of Fluellen, Jamy, and MacMorris.

In Act I we see the Archbishop of Canterbury and the Bishop of Ely rejoicing at the complete change that has come over Henry since he has become king; they praise his attitude toward politics and religion. But the churchmen realize that they can gain greater concessions if the interest of the young king is directed into foreign politics, and with this thought in mind they prepare to urge upon Henry the need for a military expedition into France. Fitting in so well with Henry Fourth's last words to his son, this idea strikes young Henry well, and he gladly receives the suggestion. He puts it up to Canterbury to pass on the justice of his making a claim to the crown of France as a pretext to invade that country, and Canterbury is only too willing to find numerous specious arguments why this expedition is the thing indicated. After a long discussion of the

Salic Law the Archbishop finally concludes that Henry has a fair claim to the crown, because of treaties made with his great-grandfather, Edward III, by the king of France after Crécy. As a matter of fact, these treaties entitled Henry only to some of the provinces of France; and these treaties had by no means been observed. If Henry had any claim at all to the French crown, it was through his great-great-grandmother, Isabella of France, wife of Edward II. A glance at the table number III will show that, except for the Salic Law, the succession to the French crown on the death of Charles IV in 1328 should have passed through Isabella to her son, Edward III, of England. But since that contingency did not appeal at all to the French mind, the French chose to place the son of Charles of Valois, brother of Philip IV, on the throne. Thus Philip of Valois succeeded his cousin Charles IV as Philip VI. His great-grandson, Charles VI of Valois, was king at the time of this play. Therefore it may easily be seen that Henry subverted his conscience to suit his ambition when he now undertook war to support any claim to the French crown. The Salic Law was based on commonsense; the French barred the crown's passing to a woman on the ground that if that woman should chance to marry abroad, as was most probable, her interest would be divided; such a contingency would not be to the best interest of France. Nor did they wish succession to the throne passing through any French princess to a foreign heir.

Henry was very careful, as he went about making preparations to invade France, not to leave his borders undefended against the Scots, who would take advantage of the least opportunity to invade England in the absence of the English king.

Next appear the ambassadors from the Dauphin bringing to Henry a gift of tennis balls, as being more suitable to the reputation Henry had made for himself in his princehood than cannon-balls. Henry recognizes the point of the French insult and replies:

> We are glad the Dauphin is so pleasant with us.
> His present and your pains we thank you for.
> When we have matched our rackets to these balls,
> We will, in France, by God's grace, play a set
> Shall strike his father's crown into the hazard.

Tell him he hath made a match with such a wrangler
That all the courts of France will be disturbed
With chaces. And we understand him well,
How he comes o'er us with our wilder days,
Not measuring what use we made of them.

We next see Henry at Southampton ready to depart for France. The plot of Richard, Earl of Cambridge, Lord Scroop, and Lord Grey to unseat Henry and place young Mortimer on the throne has been detected, though the principals of the plot themselves are unaware of the fact. Henry leads them into a shrewd trap, and they walk into it blindly. That is veritably one of the fine touches of the play. The plotters were immediately executed, and Henry was ready to embark.

In France the French King and his son, with their court, making plans to meet the English invasion, receive the ambassadors of Henry. Naturally, Henry's demands are rejected; the Dauphin shows unusual spirit in his defiance.

Before Harfleur Henry finds himself unopposed, and the city yields. He then starts on his march to Calais, but makes contact with the enemy in Picardy. Henry's forces become weakened by sickness, but he insists that even when sick one Englishman is equal to one healthy Frenchman in battle; in good health an Englishman was worth three Frenchmen. So Shakespeare lets his patriotic bias get the advantage of him. At Agincourt Henry meets the French in battle, and wins. Note the mortality lists on both sides. Though the French outnumbered the English more than five to one, success was with the English, and according to Shakespeare the British sustained very few losses. Another interesting case of patriotic bias getting the best of his common sense, for the French losses were ten thousand, the English merely twenty-five persons. Back to Calais, thence to England, and we come to the end of Act Four.

The Prologue to Act Five informs us that Henry was soon back in France with a fresh army, ready to march on Paris. In the play there is no more fighting, but royalty meets royalty to discuss the terms of peace. Historically the treaty of peace was signed at the city of Troyes, though Shakespeare has it simply in "France. A royal palace." The terms are agreed on: that Henry is to be regent of France until the death of the incumbent king, Charles VI; that at the death of Charles, Henry is to become king of France; and that Henry shall marry Katharine, daughter of the French king. Upon which note, the play ends.

We get one last glimpse of Falstaff in this play, when we learn that the old knight is sick and about to die. "The king has killed his heart," the Hostess remarks. Again she says, "Ah, poor heart! he is so shak'd of a burning quotidian tertian, that it is most lamentable to behold. Sweet men, come to him." Nym adds that "The King hath run bad humors on the knight." And Pistol with his usual Malapropian expertness with words, concludes, "His heart is fracted and corroborate." We are relieved to learn, nevertheless, that old Sir John did not remain long in confinement in Fleet Prison, and we are happy to conclude that Sir John's Hal must shortly have taken care to release his old playmate after his enforced harshness of the previous play. Then in scene III of Act II we are informed that Sir John is dead, graphically told by the Hostess, who was the first to discover that the old knight was "as cold as any stone."

Falstaff's place in the previous plays, furnisher of humor, is taken in this play by three able successors, Fluellen, Mac-Morris, and Jamy. Of course, Bardolph and Pistol must not be entirely overlooked. But Fluellen insists that King Henry of Monmouth must be very like Alexander the Great, of the same mettle, chiefly because of the similarity of the names Monmouth and Macedon. He adds that each of the two great monarchs, Alexander and Henry, killed his faithful friend: Alexander killed Cleitus; Henry, Falstaff. But these comedy characters have another function in this play beside mere comedy; for the first time in history the various parts of the British Isles were united in common allegiance to the king of the English, and Jamy, MacMorris, and Fluellen, representing Ireland, Scotland, and Wales, were all three fighting together under the standard of King Henry against a foreign foe. These three simple soldiers represent a united Great Britain, a situation hitherto unheard of.

Beside the evidences already noted of Shakespeare's patriotic bias, there is another very interesting episode in Act IV, scene IV, where Pistol has captured a French soldier. The boastful, swaggering bulldozing Pistol as compared with the cowering, frightened Frenchman portrays the poet's idea of the superiority of the Englishman over the average Frenchman. The attitude of Henry himself toward the French is one always of this same superiority, and in every utterance of his to the French prior to the scene of the treaty he is bombastic and boastful. Even in his courtship he is the overmastering Briton. Such scenes as those must have been sweet to the Englishman of Elizabeth's time, when England was blossoming into a nationalism hitherto unknown. Shakespeare knew well his audience.

The scenes written in the French language make an interesting study. How much French Shakespeare knew of course is not known. It is not uncommon for Englishmen to speak several foreign languages fluently, and there is no reason for us to assume that Shakespeare did not understand well the language of the French. In America when we find a person who speaks a foreign language easily we are astonished, because such a person is actually rare. Americans, isolated from contact with foreigners as a rule, except those who are immigrants in our midst, have small chance to pick up by conversation the language of other peoples. On our north are a people who speak our own tongue. Americans living on the southern border adjoining Mexico more often than not are acquainted with Mexican. But the average American speaks only American. This is not true on the Continent of Europe, where there are two or three dozen different languages spoken, where nations are small as to territory, and where the various nationalities mingle more easily and readily. It is not unusual for a Frenchman to speak fluently six or seven different languages. Shopkeepers in Paris find it advantageous to be able to address customers in whatever tongue is indicated by the manners and dress of the customer who approaches. It is not unnatural, therefore, that Shakespeare should have been acquainted with the French language. However, assuming that he had no knowledge of it, he might easily have written his scenes in English and have found an interpreter who changed it into French for him. Certain lapses in idiom and grammar, however, indicate, I think, that Shakespeare wrote his own French; an interpreter or translator would never have written "a les anges;" aside from a few other such slips the passages as a whole contain very commendable French for a foreigner. And their humor is on a par with that of any other scenes in the play.

Henry, like his father before him, takes occasion to soliloquize upon the cares of kingship. When Michael Williams remarks to the disguised king that the King must have a heavy load on his conscience when he will have to answer for the deaths of so many men who have died in his cause without the opportunity of having made their souls ready, Henry replies thus:

> So if a son that is by his father sent about merchandise do sinfully miscarry upon the sea, the imputation of his wickedness by your rule should be imposed upon his father that sent him; or if a servant, under his master's command transporting a sum of money, be assailed by robbers and die in many irreconciled iniquities, you may call the business of the master the author of the servant's damnation. But this is not so. The King is not bound to answer the particular endings of his soldiers, the father of his son, nor the master of his servant; for they purpose not their death, when they purpose their services. Besides there is no King, be his cause never so spotless, if it comes to the arbitrement of swords, can try it out with all unspotted soldiers.

Further on, Henry continues:

> Upon the King! let us our lives, our souls,
> Our debts, our careful wives,
> Our children, and our sins lay on the King!
> We must bear all. O hard condition,
> Twin-born with greatness, subject to the
> Breath of every fool, whose sense no more can feel
> But his own wringing! What infinite heartsease
> Must kings neglect, that private men enjoy!
> And what have kings, that privates have not too,
> Save ceremony, save general ceremony?
> And what art thou, thou idol Ceremony?
> What kind of god art thou, that suffer'st more
> Of mortal grief than do thy worshippers?
> What are thy rents? What are thy comings-in?
> O Ceremony, show me but thy worth!
> What is thy soul of adoration?
> Art thou aught else but place, degree, and form?
> Creating awe and fear in other men?

Wherein thou art less happy being feared
Than they in fearing.
What drinkst thou oft, instead of homage sweet,
But poisoned flattery? O, be sick, great greatness,
And bid thy Ceremony give thee cure!
Think'st thou the fiery fever will go out
With titles blown from adulation?
Will it give place to flexure and low bending?
Can'st thou, when thou command'st the beggar's knee,
Command the health of it? No, thou proud dream,
That play'st so subtly with a king's repose;
I am a king that find thee, and I know
'Tis not the balm, the sceptre, and the ball,
The sword, the mace, the crown imperial,
The intertissued robe of gold and pearl,
The farced title running 'fore the King,
The throne he sits on, nor the tide of pomp,
That beats upon the high shore of this world,
No, not all these, thrice-gorgeous Ceremony,—
Not all these, laid in bed majestical,
Can sleep so soundly as the wretched slave,
Who with a body filled, and vacant mind
Gets him to rest, crammed with distressful bread;
Never sees horrid night, the child of hell
But like a lackey, from the rise to set
Sweats in the eye of Phoebus, and all night
Sleeps in Elysium; next day after dawn,
Doth rise and help Hyperion to his horse;
And follows so the ever-running year,
With profitable labour, to his grave.
And, but for Ceremony, such a wretch,
Winding up days with toil and nights with sleep,
Had the forehand and vantage of a king.
The slave, a member of the country's peace,
Enjoys it, but in gross brain little wots
What watch the King keeps to maintain the peace,
Whose hours the peasant best advantages.

The responsibility of kingship seems to have rested heavily
upon the Lancastrians, whether it was because the first of
them usurped the crown, its symbol, or whether they were
naturally highly conscientious rulers. Henry Bolingbroke often
soliloquized concerning the trouble and difficulty he had as-

THE HOUSE OF YORK

Edward III
1327–1377

- Edward, the Black Prince, d. 1376
  - **Richard II** 1377–1399

- William of Hatfield

- Lionel, Duke of Clarence d. 1368
  - Phillipa, m. Edmund Mortimer, Earl of March (d. 1381)
    - Roger Mortimer, 4th Earl of March, d. 1398
      - Edmund Mortimer
      - Roger Mortimer d. 1409
      - (2) Edmund Mortimer, 5th Earl of March d. 1424
      - Elizabeth-Hotspur
    - (3) Anne-Richard, Earl of Cambridge (beheaded 1415) (1)

- John of Gaunt, Duke of Lancaster d. 1399
  - **Henry IV** 1399–1413
  - Henry V 1413–1422
    - **Henry VI** 1422–1461

- Edmund of Langley, Earl of Cambridge and Duke of York

Richard Plantagenet, Duke of York, died in battle of Wakefield (m. Cecily Nevill)

- **Edward IV** 1461–1483 — Elizabeth-Woodville (d. 1492)
  - *Edward V.* reigned 1483 d. 1483
  - Elizabeth m. Henry Tudor later *Henry VII* 1485–1509
    - *Henry VIII* 1509–1547

- Edmund, Earl of Rutland d. 1460

- George, Duke of Clarence d. 1477 m. Isabel Nevill

- *Richard III* (Duke of Gloucester) 1483–1485 m. Anne Nevill

- Richard, Duke of York d. 1483

sumed when he undertook to relieve Richard of the throne. Henry V, his son, finds royal responsibilities not what he had imagined they were; and later in *Henry VI* we have that weak son of a strong father yearning for the quiet bookishness of a remote monastery. One comes to wonder if Shakespeare were not perhaps painting with a purpose a portrait of the English throne as being not what the layman might think it to be. Still, as we have said before, it is very easy to read into Shakespeare theories the poet himself perhaps never dreamed of. Verily Shakespeare would have been super-great if he had the genius the composite of his criticism has imputed to him. On the other hand, he may have been all that they have said of him, and more.

CHAPTER VIII

Henry VI, 1422-1471

Henry VI. 1422—Dethroned 1461—Died 1471.
Born, 1421; married, 1446, Margaret of Anjou.
Kings of France: Charles VI, died 1422; Charles VII, died 1461

The reign of Henry V was noteworthy for its lack of outstanding events such as are usually recorded by historians;
except for his campaigns in France and the Treaty of Troyes,
there is little of interest to the student of history who seeks
for great battles and great political upheavals. It may be, however, that this fact is one of the fundamental reasons for the
greatness of Henry's reign. His affairs were so well ordered, his
administration so wise, that the march of events moved
smoothly on without complications such as marked the reign,
for instance, of John. By the same token the reign of his son,
Henry VI, furnishes a surfeit for the recording historian, and
his incumbency was marked by upheaval after upheaval, by
struggle after struggle, by mistake after mistake. The strength
of Henry V made for order and progress; the weakness of
Henry VI produced chaos and turmoil throughout his long
reign of thirty-nine years.

Henry VI was an infant nine months old when his father
died, and the affairs of the kingdom were administered during his minority by a protector and council. That fact in itself
naturally set the stage for dissensions of all kinds, and they
were not slow to develop. The young king's uncle, John, Duke
of Bedford, was made regent, with the provision that he
should be protector so long as his duties allowed him to remain in England; but when it became necessary for Bedford
to go into France for the conduct of the affairs of the provinces,

it was agreed that Humphrey, Duke of Gloucester, younger uncle of the king, should serve as protector of the realm at home. The council that guided the affairs of state was composed of Gloucester as chairman, and of five prelates, one duke, five earls, and five barons. As it turned out, Bedford was compelled to spend most of the time in France, and Gloucester was therefore most of the time protector.

Bedford very wisely managed affairs in France, but in spite of his care the condition of France grew more and more unfavorable to the growth of English prestige in that country. Charles VI had died in 1422, and the succession had passed to the Dauphin as Charles VII, which of course was directly in contravention to the terms of the Treaty of Troyes. So at this point Bedford decided that it was time to reassert the power of England in France, and laid siege to the city of Orleans. As the siege went on without marked progress, there appeared on the scene a girl named Jeanne D'Arc, daughter of a peasant of Domrémy, who believed that she had a divine mission to lead her countrymen to victory over the English and to crown Charles VII as king of France at Rheims. Her energy, enthusiasm, and pertinacity fired the spirits of the French with the result that shortly the siege of Orleans was raised, Suffolk and Talbot, English leaders, were defeated, and within the year Charles VII was actually crowned at Rheims. Then came a reaction; the English recovered their morale, the French allowed jealousy to divide them, and the English finally captured Jeanne D'Arc at Compiègne in May, 1430. Then the spell was broken. She was tried and condemned as a witch by a court of Norman and Burgundian prelates, presided over by the Bishop of Beauvais. She was burned as a witch at Rouen in May, 1431, and her ashes were thrown into the Seine.

English affairs in France were more or less at a standstill for a while, until in 1435 two events brought matters to a head. In that year on September 14 Bedford died, and on September 21 the Duke of Burgundy, hitherto an ally of the English, went over to the French side. From that point dates the rapid decline of English power in France. During the thirteen years of Bedford's administration abroad Gloucester had been causing trouble at home. Several times Bedford had been forced to return home in order to settle quarrels and political upsets caused by Gloucester's poor judgment. The chief quarrel in which Gloucester was engaged was with Henry Beaufort, great-uncle to the young king, Bishop of Winchester. Throughout these quarrels, mostly based on jealousy and political intrigue, Beaufort had the confidence of the country at large, and parliament was on his side; but Gloucester had the support of the London mob, with whom Beaufort was unpopular. Beaufort lost some of his prestige when he accepted from the Pope an appointment to the Cardinalate.

Upon Bedford's death the regency of France was bestowed by Parliament upon young Richard, Duke of York, and the captaincy of Calais was entrusted to Gloucester. But they were able to accomplish nothing, for Paris was lost. In the meantime at home a strong feeling was growing that England was not strong enough to maintain her French policy, and that it was a losing game in face of such strong French opposition to the policy; the chief advocate of letting France go was Henry Beaufort, while the chief defender of the idea that France belonged to England and must be kept was Gloucester, who was the natural mouthpiece of the war-like nobility and the junkers. But Gloucester had grown powerful, chiefly through his popularity with the Londoners, and had managed somehow to win for himself the reputation for chivalry and the title of "The Good", a name not at all agreeing with his exploits in war nor with the events of his private life.

Henry VI reached his majority in 1442. He had grown up a courteous gentleman, well trained in chivalry, literature, and in the art of government, but he lacked the moral fibre required to lead a nation in time of national emergency. He was morally sound, inclined to be religious, accomplished to a high degree, but unfitted by nature to be a successful king. This incompetence was unnoticed while the government was in the hands of able men like Bedford, Beaufort, and Gloucester, but when Henry himself took control of state affairs, his inadequacy soon declared itself.

In 1444 an embassy headed by William de la Pole, Earl of Suffolk, went to France in order to consider terms for an Anglo-French agreement. The result of the embassy was a truce for two years, and an arrangement that Henry should marry the niece of the queen of Charles VII, Margaret, daughter of René,

Duke of Anjou and Count of Provence, titular king of Naples and Jerusalem. The marriage took place in 1446. To many this alliance was excellent, but not to Humphrey, Duke of Gloucester. Gloucester was opposed to it on three grounds: first because it was a triumph for those who favored peace, especially Henry Beaufort; second, because the marriage was contrived by Suffolk, whom Gloucester hated; and third, because the birth of an heir to Henry would bar Gloucester's own hopes of succession to the crown, since he stood next in succession after the death of Bedford.

In 1447 parliament met at Bury St. Edmunds. When Gloucester arrived to attend parliament he was arrested by the Earl of Salisbury, September 18. On the 23rd Gloucester died. The manner of his death is not known, but the rumor soon got abroad that he had been murdered in his lodgings by Suffolk; some even said that Margaret had been an instigator of the crime. But Margaret was at that time just eighteen years old, and it is doubtful that she should have had a hand in the affair. In six weeks from the death of Gloucester, Cardinal Beaufort also died, leaving behind him a reputation as being the greatest of the House of Beaufort, and next to Cardinal Wolsey, the greatest ecclesiastic England has produced.

With Bedford, Gloucester, and Winchester gone, Suffolk soon maneuvered himself into power. From the beginning he had insinuated himself into the confidence of Margaret; Somerset was busied in France with his command; in 1447 Richard of York was created lord-lieutenant of Ireland, a position which kept him away from the center of affairs; thus Suffolk had things entirely his own way. His first action was to sign away the provinces of Anjou and Maine to René, as had been agreed when Henry married Margaret. This event caused very bitter protests in England, and started a trend of unpopularity for Suffolk. In addition there occurred several reverses to the English army in France, all of which were blamed on Suffolk. The result was that Suffolk soon faced impeachment, and Henry ordered Suffolk to leave England for five years, until the people should somewhat forget their attitude toward him. On April 30, 1450, Suffolk set sail; but his ship was intercepted near Calais, and Suffolk was taken off, placed in a small boat, decapitated, and his body thrown on the shore of Kent.

The next important event of Henry's reign was Cade's Rebellion. Jack Cade was an Irish retainer of Sir Thomas Dacre. Like so many of these peasants' uprisings, the movement had its inception in Kent. Cade affirmed that he was a Mortimer, cousin of the Duke of York, and that he was fighting in the interests of York. He advanced on London, giving as the grievances of the rebels the loss of France, unjust taxation, and the ill government of the country. Cade entered London on July 3, 1450, and was well received by the inhabitants; the rebels captured Lord Say, Henry's treasurer, and executed him. But the peasants were disappointed in not finding some noblemen to join them, and disheartened, soon began to disperse. Cade kept a few men with him, however, and was finally forced to flee in disguise. Soon he was captured in Kent and was slain by Alexander Iden, sheriff of Kent.

One by one Henry had lost his most capable advisers. At this juncture Richard, Duke of York, concluded that it was expedient for him to begin putting into execution his plans to increase his own influence at court. He therefore collected 4000 men, came to London, demanded of the king a hearing, and found the king willing to listen to reason. Henry declared he had never associated York with Cade's uprising, and still considered him his faithful friend and subject. But just now Somerset came back to England. The next three years were spent in rivalry and struggle between York and Somerset for ascendancy at the court, with Margaret favoring Somerset since York was now next in succession to the crown in case Henry should have no son.

But English affairs in France were going from bad to worse, much to the chagrin of Somerset, on whom the blame for such mismanagement was laid. In 1452 a force of five thousand men was dispatched by Somerset to Bordeaux under command of Sir John Talbot, and in the next July, on the 17th of the month, Talbot attacked the French at Castillon. He was greatly outnumbered, with the result that he was disastrously defeated, and himself and his son were killed in action. This loss left nothing to the English in France save Calais.

Then King Henry became very ill. Whether he inherited madness from his grandfather, Charles VI, or whether worry over conditions in his kingdom drove him mad, the fact remains that his mind became completely unhinged. Following upon news of the king's mental incapacity came also the announcement that Margaret had given birth to a son. This event changed the whole political complexion. It was necessary that a regent be chosen to administer the government during the impotence of the king; Somerset had become so unpopular that he was out of the question; the outcome was that York was chosen and he immediately assumed the reins of government. In the next year York became officially the protector; he immediately set about to stabilize the government, to remove evil practices, and to reform the administration. He filled all offices with men on whom he could rely; he appointed Salisbury chancellor, Worcester treasurer, and Warwick a member of the council. At the same time he arrested Somerset and held him in the Tower.

But in December, 1455, Henry gradually recovered from his disaffection, and insisted again on assuming the government. His first act was to free Somerset, who again assumed his place of ascendancy on the council. York had to resign his post of protector, and all of his appointees lost their jobs. Not only that, but a parliament was called for the purpose of taking steps against "the king's enemies." York knew to whom that phrase referred, and decided to take the initiative. He summoned Salisbury and Warwick to his aid, marched to London, but was met on the way by Somerset and the king at St. Albans, and a fight ensued in which Henry was wounded and Somerset and Clifford were killed.

This left York practically supreme. He restored his friends to official positions. And in October, 1455, Henry again suffered a mental lapse, and York again became protector. But Henry recovered in January, 1456, and the old intrigues started again, this time with Margaret taking matters in her own hands. She immediately removed York's friends from their positions of power, and in 1459 felt herself strong enough to take stronger measures still. She collected an army of 50,000 men, determined to attack York and his friends and put an end to his aspirations. York was joined by Salisbury and Warwick, who had altogether only 20,000 followers. They met at Ludford, but panic seized York's forces, and York was forced to flee to Ireland, while Salisbury, Warwick, and York's oldest son, Edward, Earl of March, succeeded in escaping to Calais. This left Margaret for the moment in full possession of affairs in England.

Margaret proceeded to take immediate steps to attaint the rebellious nobles and to seize their property. York and his adherents returned to England with increased forces, attacked a Lancastrian force led by Henry himself at Northampton, captured Henry, and marched on to London. Margaret and her young son had escaped. Parliament convened in October, 1460, and Richard of York appeared openly to claim the crown as heir of Richard II. Richard was moving too fast now for his followers, and they did not support his claim, thinking too strongly of their oaths of allegiance to Henry as king. Therefore the lords did not approve. A compromise was arrived at whereby York was declared heir to the throne at the death of Henry VI and was given the title of Protector and Prince of Wales. This action was approved by parliament and accepted by Henry.

But Queen Margaret was not one to stand idly by and see her son thus deprived of his hereditary rights. She collected her forces, met the Yorkists at Wakefield, caught York unguarded and slew him. His second son, Rutland, was also killed, and Salisbury was captured.

Edward, Earl of March, oldest son of the slain Duke of York, now assumed his father's title and ambitions. Margaret had an army of 40,000 marching southwards; Warwick with 30,000 men was at St. Albans, standing between Margaret and London; Edward with 10,000 men was in the valley of the Severn; and Pembroke with a body of Welshmen was threatening Edward's rear. Edward turned on Pembroke at Mortimer's Cross on February 2, 1461, and defeated him; Pembroke's father, Owen Tudor, was slain. But in the meantime Margaret met Warwick at St. Albans and administered to him a severe defeat, Warwick himself barely managing to escape with a few of his men to join Edward. For a while it seemed that Margaret had succeeded in putting the Yorkists out of the way entirely, and that her road to London was open. But she dallied, and the Londoners, hearing that Warwick and Edward were still in the field, decided to turn their assistance in that direction; and the next day Warwick and Edward entered London.

The first time York made claim to the crown his move was received with little ardor in London. But gradually the people had come to regard Margaret as a menace and now they were ready to disown Margaret and her puppet-husband Henry in favor of Edward. Therefore, on Sunday, March 9, 1461, the Bishop of Exeter addressed the soldiers and presented Edward's claim to the throne; his speech was loudly applauded. The sequel, of course, was a summoning of the members of the Yorkist party, in a meeting of which Edward was formally elected king and was proclaimed as Edward IV.

The next move of the Yorkists was to pursue Margaret and Henry. They came in contact with the Lancastrian forces on March 29, 1461, at Towton, and succeeded in utterly putting them to rout. Margaret and Henry took refuge in Scotland. In 1465 Henry was captured and confined in the Tower, while Margaret made her way to France. Everything now seemed smooth for Edward and his family.

Warwick, who had been Edward's staunch adherent throughout, now undertook to cement friendly relations with France for the new regime by an alliance by marriage with the French royal house. Accordingly Edward allowed Warwick to go to France in order to make arrangements for Edward's marriage with Bona, sister of the wife of the French king. But on September 28, 1464, within a week of the date arranged for Warwick's meeting with the French king, Edward suddenly announced that there was no further use for negotiations, since he had already been married since the first of May to Lady Elizabeth Gray. This breach of trust was an insult to Warwick, who immediately turned against Edward and made an alliance with Margaret, who was also in France petitioning the king of France to take up her quarrel with the Yorkists; and the king of France, Louis XI, feeling the insult offered by Edward to his sister-in-law, decided to assist Margaret by furnishing her with an army to invade England. Warwick sealed his alliance with Margaret by marrying his daugher Anne to Margaret's son, Edward, former Prince of Wales. For the next seven years history is concerned chiefly with the duel between Warwick, "the king-maker", and young King Edward whom Warwick had wished to keep under his thumb, but who had broken loose too soon.

The lady whom Edward had married was the daughter of Jacquetta of Luxembourg, Duchess of Bedford, and her second husband, Richard Woodville, Lord Rivers. Elizabeth had previously married John Grey, who had been killed fighting with the Lancastrians against the Yorkists at the second battle of St. Albans. Edward immediately proceeded to elevate her kinsmen to positions of importance in the realm in order to create a counterpoise against the Neville family, chief member of which was the Earl of Warwick. He married every marriageable member of his wife's family to members of the peerage; he made his father-in-law lord treasurer, later raised him to an earldom, and finally created him constable of England; he gave the queen's brothers and son positions of influence in the government.

Warwick in the meantime worked to effect a marriage between his daughter, Isabel, and George, Duke of Clarence, Edward's younger brother, an alliance Edward peremptorily forbade; but Clarence went to Calais, married Isabel Neville, and joined Warwick against his brother the king. They came to England, found Edward unprepared, and took him prisoner. Edward was so popular, however, that Warwick soon found it expedient to release him.

In 1470 Warwick again made plans to invade England, in order to restore Henry to the throne. Margaret remained in France. Warwick landed in England, gathered his friends, found Edward again unprepared. Edward this time was forced to flee to the protection of Burgundy, and Warwick had command of the situation. The king-maker entered London, released Henry from the Tower, and placed him again on the throne. Clarence, all the while, kept in communication with Edward, all the time having had intentions of deserting Warwick and joining forces with his brother. Edward again landed at Ravenspur on March 15, 1471, with a motley force of English exiles, German mercenaries, and French loaned him by the Duke of Burgundy, marched on to London in the absence of Warwick, declared himself king again, and then proceeded against the rebel Earl. He met Warwick at Barnet, on April 14, and with the aid of his brother Richard and of Clarence, who now had joined him, he defeated his enemy. Warwick was slain.

Margaret was on her way to England with her forces when Warwick was struggling at Barnet, but she had been delayed. She soon landed at Weymouth and marched toward Edward. The armies met at Tewkesbury on May 4, 1471. Edward was completely victorious, and in the contest Margaret's son, Edward, was killed, and Margaret herself taken prisoner. Edward returned to London, where on the day of his entry into the city Henry VI died in the Tower, presumably by the hand of Edward's youngest brother, Richard of Gloucester. Margaret was released by the terms of the Treaty of Picquigny, signed with King Louis of France. She returned to France, and never again crossed over into England.

The First Part of King Henry VI.
The Play

Historic Time: September, 1422-May 22, 1443
Dramatic Time: 8 days.
Place: England and France.
Purpose: To portray the fortunes of York and Lancaster.
Date of Composition: 1590

Of all the historical plays the *First Part of Henry VI* is perhaps the least interesting to the casual reader. No great character struts across the stage here as Bolingbroke in *Richard II* or Hotspur in *Henry IV* or Gloucester in *Richard III*. No wonderful reaches of poetry occur, such as may be found in *Henry IV* and *Henry V*. No dramatic events hold the reader breathless; the plot becomes very thin. The chief virtue of the first of the *Henry VI* trilogy is that it is in the nature of an introduction to the action and events of the Wars of the Roses, which forms the nucleus of the complication for the other plays of the trilogy.

There has been much argument concerning the authorship of these three plays. There are those who think Shakespeare wrote the second and third parts, but not the first; others believe that Shakespeare had his hand in the appearance of three previous dramatic productions based on the period of Henry VI, and that the present three plays are his own re-writing of what he had formerly only assisted in. The material for the plots of the three parts of *Henry VI* was drawn from

Holinshed's *Chronicles*. The historical facts thus obtained were used very freely by the poet; for instance, the calamities reported by the Messenger in the first act of the first part as having occurred prior to the date of the funeral of Henry V in 1422 are either unhistorical, as in the case of the loss of Orleans and Poictiers, which did not at that time belong to the English, or are antedated by from seven to twenty-nine years, as in the case of the loss of Rheims, Guysors, Paris, and Guienne. Too, the death of Talbot in the play antedates the capture of Joan of Arc, while as a matter of history Talbot lived until 1453, and Joan of Arc was burned in 1431. The defection of Burgundy did not actually occur until four years after the death of Joan. Again, of course, the explanation is that the dramatist used his material for the best dramatic effect. In that case, what does a little deviation from history matter?

At the beginning we see the nobles of the realm mourning the passing of Henry V, calling upon his spirit to be with them in the troublous times they see ahead. Messengers arrive one after another bringing evil news of losses in France. The scene shifts quickly to Orléans, where the English armies lie around the city in siege. Jeanne D'Arc appears on the scene, introducing herself by means of an exercise of supernatural power in being able to recognise the Dauphin whom she had never previously seen. She gives her life history, and challenges Charles to a fight in order to prove still further her uncanny power. Convinced of her genuineness, they commission her to lead the French out of their emergency.

With unusual nimbleness the scene shifts again to London, where we are introduced to the quarrel between Gloucester and Winchester. But the shift is short-lived, for we are quickly taken back to France, and find Joan la Pucelle at work, instilling new courage into the despairing French, fighting hand-to-hand with distinguished Englishmen and defeating them, and finally succeeding in driving the English from the environs of Orléans.

Then follows the episode where Talbot outwits the Countess of Auvergne, a scene that has no earthly reason other than to define the prowess of the great English leader.

Perhaps the best scene of the whole play comes next, the Temple Garden scene in London, the real beginning of the Wars of the Roses. Somerset, Suffolk, Warwick, Richard, Duke of York, and others are there. Richard asserts his position, calling upon those who favor him to stand beside him. Warwick is called upon to umpire the quarrel. He hesitates:

> Between two hawks, which flies the higher pitch;
> Between two dogs, which hath the deeper mouth;
> Between two blades, which hath the better temper;
> Between two horses, which doth bear him best;
> Between two girls, which hath the merriest eye;
> I have perhaps some shallow spirit of judgment;
> But in these nice sharp quillets of the law,
> Good faith, I am no wiser than a daw.

So the white roses and the red are plucked. Richard defends the honor of his father and of his house, and forms an agreement with Warwick that stood him in good stead on a later day.

Richard Plantagenet goes next to visit his uncle, Edmund Mortimer, to learn from him some of his family history. The Mortimer in this scene is Edmund Mortimer, 5th Earl of March, who as a child was kept under surveillance by Henry IV, but to whom his estates and freedom were restored under Henry V. The story he here relates to Richard is essentially correct. His death occurred in 1425. Mortimer states that by his mother he was derived from Lionel, when as a matter of fact, it was through his grandmother, Philippa, daughter of Lionel, that he could trace his line to Edward III. Edmund Mortimer, Earl of March, was son of Roger, Earl of March, who died in 1398. This Edmund was brother of Anne Mortimer, wife of Richard, Earl of Cambridge and Duke of York, the parents of the present Richard Plantagenet. On the death of Edmund, Richard fell heir to his title of Earl of March, which passed to Richard's oldest son, Edward, later King Edward IV.

The third act begins with the continuance of the quarrel between Gloucester and Winchester. The Duke of Gloucester, Protector of the Realm, was youngest son of Henry IV, and was therefore uncle to King Henry VI. Winchester was the king's great-uncle, son of John of Gaunt by his third wife, Katherine Swynford. Winchester's name was Henry Beaufort; he was made Bishop of Lincoln in 1398, Bishop of Winchester in 1405, and became a Cardinal of the Church of Rome in 1426. Winchester was by far the ablest man in the kingdom at this time, and had the support of the nobles in his attempts to repress the ambitions of Gloucester. Shakespeare rather prefers Gloucester to Winchester in his portrayal, but he does so following Holinshed. As the quarrel goes on, the king undertakes to act as peacemaker, and succeeds in patching up a kind of truce, which the Bishop promises himself to disregard. York is restored to his former titles and estates. Back in France the action continues around Rouen, and care is taken to insert a scene depicting the cowardice of Sir John Fastolfe. Joan la Pucelle persuades Burgundy to desert the English, to align himself with his countrymen. That point is naturally the climax of the play.

The third act ends with the English court assembled in Paris, and the knighting of Talbot for his heroic services. One speech by King Henry is worthy of note. He says:

> When I was young, as yet I am not old,
> I do remember how my father said
> A stouter champion never handled sword.

Henry is thus made out far more precocious than history or nature would justify, since he was only nine months old when his father died. With the coronation of Henry in Paris the scene comes to an end, the action continuing on into the following act.

Next we see Talbot betrayed at Bordeaux. The blame for the defeat of Talbot is placed by York upon Somerset, who purposely dallied that such an event might come about. Somerset, however, makes excuses, claiming that Talbot rashly undertook too much. Historically, he is right.

In the last act Winchester is made a cardinal, and arrangements are being sought whereby peace may be concluded, sealed by the marriage of the king. Suffolk woos Margaret as proxy for Henry, and she accepts. Shakespeare here takes occasion to develop the Lancelot-Guinevere motif, which plays so important a part in the next play. Joan la Pucelle is condemned to die as a witch; Shakespeare has no concern for the reputation of the martyred girl. However, rightly to appreciate his treatment of her, it must be remembered that the blame for all the English losses in France may be placed on her, that she was regarded by the English as no saint, and that Shakespeare was writing of her only one hundred and fifty years after she had done such incalculable harm to the English prestige. Moreover, the nationalistic attitude of the English in Elizabeth's time demanded that she be made an object of contempt rather than one of eulogy.

The play ends as Suffolk goes to France to bring Margaret to England to become Queen. The action thus is unfinished. This naturally links the *First Part of Henry VI* to the one which immediately follows, as we see Gloucester opposing with all his nature the alliance which brings England no security, no advantage, but really a severe loss of three of her best possessions in France. Gloucester is the patriot, bemoaning a step that must work England harm; actually, however, it was his hostility to Suffolk rather than his patriotism that prompted such an attitude.

The Second Part of King Henry VI.
The Play

Historic Time: April 22, 1445-May 22, 1455
Dramatic Time: 14 days
Place: England
Purpose: To continue the fortunes of York and Lancaster
Date of composition: 1591

The Second Part of King Henry VI begins with the marriage and coronation of Margaret on the 22nd of April, 1445. A very imposing scene Shakespeare makes of it, with all the great of the land composing the august assembly. Gloucester is there, still functioning as Lord Protector. His enemy, the Bishop of Winchester, is there, still agitating the quarrel which the king had tried in vain to quell. Richard of York is there, keeping his plans as yet to himself, but plotting, nevertheless, to overthrow the weakling now sitting on the throne and to take that uncomfortable seat himself. Warwick, the great kingmaker, is there, silent now, but throwing his trememdous influence later to the support of the Duke of York. Suffolk is

THE FAMILY OF THE BEAUFORTS.

Edward III
|
John of Gaunt (4th son)—Katherine Swynford
|
+---------------------------+---------------------------+---------------------------+
| | |
John Beaufort,   Henry Beaufort,   Thomas
cr. Earl of Somerset, 1397 Bishop of Lincoln,
d. 1410. m. Margaret Holland Bishop of Winchester
| 1405
| Cardinal, 1426.
| d. 1447
|
+---------------------------+---------------------------+---------------------------+
| | |
Edmund Beaufort   Joan Beaufort,   Margaret
cr. Duke of Somerset,   m. James I of
1448. Killed at   Scotland
St. Albans, 1455
|
+---------------------------+---------------------------+
| |
Henry, 2nd   Edmund, called   John, slain at
Duke of Somerset,   Duke of Somerset,   Tewkesbury, 1471
d. 1464   beheaded at
                            Tewkesbury, 1471

John Beaufort,
cr. Duke of Somerset,
1443. d. 1444
|
Margaret Beaufort,
m. Edmund Tudor
m. Sir Henry Stafford (2)
m. Thomas, Lord Stanley (3)
|
Henry Tudor,
later *Henry VII*

there, the man who had made himself a power in the kingdom and had increased that power by his influence over the Queen herself. The very atmosphere is charged with the electricity of ambition and hatred, faction opposing faction, until we can feel the inevitable clash that soon must occur. Something is going to happen.

Gloucester is called upon to read the articles of agreement between the French and the English consummated by the marriage of Henry and Margaret. Very dramatically he drops the paper, when he comes to the item concerning the giving away of Anjou and Maine; he can read no further, for emotion has dimmed his eyes. Thereupon Winchester takes up the paper and reads, at the conclusion of which the king, confessing himself well satisfied, withdraws from the assembly. Immediately there is a general denouncement of the terms, friends and foes alike joining in the accusations against Suffolk for having sponsored so evil an agreement. Old grudges are remembered soon, however, and hot words follow between Gloucester and Winchester. When all have retired save York, he soliloquizing states his case:

> Then, York, be still a while, till time do serve.
> Watch thou and wake when others be asleep.
> Then will I raise aloft the milk-white rose,
> With whose sweet smell the air shall be perfumed,
> And in my standard bear the arms of York,
> To grapple with the house of Lancaster;
> And, force perforce, I'll make him yield the crown,
> Whose bookish rule hath pulled fair England down.

Eleanor Cobham, wife of Gloucester, tells her husband a dream she had dreamed concerning her ambitions. He reprimands her, but her ambition outruns her discretion, and she plots against the royal house with some so-called sorcerers. A trap is laid for her by Suffolk and Margaret, into which she walks easily. Thus they aim to strike at her husband. Eleanor is accused of consorting with witches and is condemned to do penance. In the meantime, York and Warwick form an alliance, the end of which is the removal of Henry from the throne and his supplanting by York.

Christmas of the year sees Parliament meeting at Bury St. Edmund's, a move of Suffolk's to get Gloucester away from London, where his chief strength lay with the Londoners. When Gloucester arrives, he is immediately arrested on a charge of treason, and finds that all have turned against him. He is committed to Winchester for safe-keeping. In the meantime York is sent to Ireland to suppress an uprising there. He resolves to use his resources there to organize for himself sufficient strength for his purposes at home. Also he tells us of his plans to promote Cade's rebellion; the outcome of that will be his barometer of the feeling toward him of the common people, who, by the way, are growing more and more influential in the affairs of state. Gloucester is found lying dead in his bed, and suspicion attaches necessarily to Suffolk. The commons, with whom Gloucester was very popular, instantly began demanding revenge on Suffolk; Warwick openly accuses Suffolk of having brought about the old Duke's death. The only thing remaining for the king is to banish Suffolk, and this he orders. And soon the Bishop of Winchester dies.

Suffolk leaves for France but is forcibly removed from his ship and is slain. Cade's Rebellion gets under way. Queen Margaret is of course broken-hearted over Suffolk's end, with whom Shakespeare would have us believe she had conducted an illicit affair. There is quite an ironical touch in Shakespeare's description of the capture of Lord Say, Treasurer of the Realm, by the rebels of Cade. He is accused by the rabble of increasing the taxes and "selling the towns in France." He has:

> Most traitorously corrupted the youth of the realm in erecting a grammar school; and whereas, before, our forefathers had no other books but the score and the tally, thou hast caused printing to be used, and, contrary to the King, his crown and dignity, thou hast built a paper mill. It will be proved to thy face that thou hast men about thee that usually talk of a noun and a verb, and such abominable words as no Christian ear can endure to hear.

When Lord Say makes the mistake of quoting Latin to them, his captors shout, "Away with him, away with him! he speaks Latin." The rebels then conduct their prisoner away to be beheaded. But Buckingham and Clifford by their oratory convince the rabble that they are entirely wrong, and Cade is left to flee for his life. Some will say that here Shakespeare takes a fling at the shallowness of the commons; Cade himself remarks: "Was ever feather so lightly blown to and fro as this multitude?" At any rate, Cade's Rebellion is over, and a price is put on the leader's head. Later he is discovered in Kent and slain.

York has succeeded in raising an army in Ireland, and approaches London. He is met by Buckingham who assures him that Somerset is under arrest in the Tower, upon which information York dismisses his forces. He then discovers that he has been hoodwinked, that Somerset is free and in power. Salisbury and Warwick come to York's support, upon which York declares openly his intention of claiming the crown. The opposing armies then meet on the field of St. Alban's, where the Yorkists come off victorious, Somerset being slain. The King withdraws to London, whither York and his followers hasten immediately, and upon that note of suspense the play ends.

Out of the mass of characters who take part in this play there emerge a few who warrant further consideration because of the part they play in the sequel. Chief of these is Warwick. The Earl of Warwick was a member of the powerful Nevill family, which for many generations had strengthened itself by a series of fortunate marriages. It now held among its members at least twelve of the thirty-six peerages that existed in England. Richard Nevill, the present Earl of the play, had married the daughter of the 5th Earl of Warwick, Richard Beauchamp, and through his wife had come into the title and estates of the Beauchamps, which made him the wealthiest landholder in England. He was the grandson of Ralph Nevill, Earl of Westmoreland who married Joan Beaufort, daughter of John of Gaunt. Because of his immense wealth and his family connections he had become the baron of most consequence in all England. He owned over a hundred and fifty manors and fifteen strong castles; contemporary historians speak of the lavish manner in which he held open house and furnished enormous banquets to the countryside. The number of his retainers was enormous. His power and influence grew to such an extent that at his prime whichever side he should choose to support would surely win; it was said of him that he could make and unmake kings at his will, a power that gave him the sobriquet of "Kingmaker."

Somerset came to be one of the most important personages

of this period. He was Edmund Beaufort, grandson of John of Gaunt and Katharine Swynford, nephew of Henry Beaufort, Bishop of Winchester and later Cardinal. Somerset acquired the title of Duke of Somerset on the death in 1444 of his older brother, John Beaufort. His influence at court and in the political arrangement of the time was very great; particularly was he hostile to Richard, Duke of York, and by his intrigues delayed the progress of York to the English throne to a marked degree. His wife, Eleanor Beauchamp, was sister of Anne, wife of the Earl of Warwick.

But one of the most interesting characters, so far as the sequel is concerned, is young Richard of York, son of Richard, Duke of York. He is mentioned in this play merely as Richard, son of the Duke of York, but he was destined to became Richard, Duke of Gloucester, and eventually King Richard III. He appears with his brother Edward, later King Edward IV, only in the last act of this play; Shakespeare has them supporting valiantly their father before St. Alban's, when Clifford defies York in favor of Henry VI. Richard speaks up boldly when he is called upon to speak, and Clifford turns on him with wrath:

> Hence, heap of wrath, foul indigested lump, As crooked in thy manner as thy shape!

This is our first introduction to the hunchback who later is pictured by Shakespeare, with the possible exception of Iago, as one of the greatest villains in literature. And toward the end of the play young Richard fights with Somerset and kills him; and Salisbury states at the close of the play that three times today he owes his life to Richard, who fought off his adversaries. For a boy born in 1452, fighting in a battle in 1455, that is great praise.

The Third Part of King Henry VI
The Play

Historic Time: May, 1455 - May, 1475
Dramatic Time: 20 days.
Place: England
Purpose: To portray the victory of the House of York.
Date of Composition: 1592.

Immediately after the battle of St. Albans the rival parties assembled in the House of Parliament. When King Henry enters the Hall he finds York sitting on the throne. After much bickering King Henry agrees that if York will be lenient and allow him to reign for the rest of his life, he will gladly sign away the succession to York or his heirs. Soon Margaret is observed approaching, and Henry with Exeter fears to meet her, since he has recently agreed to the disinheriting of their son, young Edward of Wales. Nor can Henry be blamed for wishing to avoid her; she has heard the news and was now come to upbraid him. Through it all the reader cannot but feel a sort of pity for the helpless king, who tries so hard to do right, who hates the fighting and the wrangling and the bloodshed of which lately he has been the center, who prefers soft words and friendliness to armies and threats and ambitions. Margaret goes to join her army, determined now that since the king has let her down she will take matters in her own hands.

York is persuaded by his sons and friends to disregard the terms of the agreement he has just made with Henry, and to set about immediately to gain the crown. The rival forces meet at Wakefield. Rutland, second son of the Duke of York, is captured and slain by Clifford. The battle of Wakefield was fought on December 29, 1460. Rutland was born in 1443, and was at this time seventeen years old. Shakespeare portrays him as much younger, but in reality he was six years older than Clarence and nine years older than Richard. Margaret and her forces succeed in capturing York, and after making sport of him by placing on his head a paper crown they slay him. The battle ends in a complete rout of the Yorkists.

Two months later, on February 2, 1461, the battle of Mortimer's Cross was fought. Shakespeare has the time of scene I of Act II following immediately that of the preceding scene. The sons of York learn of the death of their father, and are joined by Warwick. Edward assumes the title of his dead father, and with it his ambitions. They determine to push more closely after Margaret, asserting that it is she against whom their energies are bent rather than against the good and pious king. Even the Yorkists can find no hatred for Henry.

At Towton on March 29, 1461, another battle was fought, with victory resting with the Yorkists. Clifford was killed. All seemed clear now for Edward, and he looks toward London. Richard becomes Duke of Gloucester and his brother George the Duke of Clarence.

Shakespeare next presents Edward as King Edward IV, and following Holinshed depicts Edward's courtship of Lady Grey. A strange courtship, almost as strange as that later courtship of Gloucester and Anne Warwick. News is brought that Henry has been taken; he is sent to the Tower. In this scene we get too the first real intimation of the ambition of young Gloucester, as he fervently hopes that no issue may result from Edward's alliance with Lady Grey to stand between him and the throne which he desires. In a long soliloquy he unfolds his plans—a long character-revealing speech prophetic of the Gloucester who appears so vividly in the next play.

But Warwick has gone to France to arrange for a marriage between Edward and the sister of the French Queen, Bona. At the same time Margaret is there, suing the French King Louis for assistance in removing Edward from the throne and reinstating her husband. Louis is wavering, until news comes that Edward has repudiated Warwick, has already married Lady Grey, no more than a commoner. Louis feels the insult thus offered his sister-in-law, and Warwick is disgusted with the lustful Edward whom he has been so instrumental in placing on the throne. So Warwick, Louis, and Margaret combine against Edward, planning to raise an army to attack him. Naturally this point marks the climax of the play.

In London the new queen is crowned. The brothers of the king resent Edward's preferment of the Queen's family, a schism that divided the York family for many years and caused jealousy long after Edward himself was gone. News comes of the triple alliance against him, and Edward makes ready for war. Clarence goes over to Warwick's side. The opposing forces meet near the town of Warwick and Edward is uncrowned by Warwick and taken prisoner. He escapes to France. In the meantime Margaret and Warwick enter London, restore Henry to the throne, and for a time the Lancastrians are again in the saddle. But not for long. Edward returns, gathers recruits by the way, enters London, and Act IV ends with Henry being taken back to the Tower.

At Barnet, Easter Day, 1471, Edward met Warwick's forces.

Clarence deserts to Edward's side, the battle goes against the old Kingmaker, and Warwick is slain. The victorious Yorkists now turn toward Margaret, who has her army at Tewkesbury. On May 4 the two armies made contact. The son of Henry and Margaret is slain on the field of battle by Gloucester, and Margaret is taken prisoner. She is sent back to France as the play ends.

Shakespeare has followed history very closely in these three plays of *Henry VI*. There are a number of marked deviations, of course, but nearly all of them may be explained by dramatic necessity. His treatment of Joan of Arc, his making Henry VI older in the first play than he actually was, his treatment likewise of the sons of York, and a few similar changes are all of which we may justly accuse him. In nearly every detail he followed history as revealed to him by Holinshed. In character portrayal, too, he has been very true, except in the case of Joan of Arc and of Humphrey, Duke of Gloucester. Aside from those two, nearly every character in the three plays resembles the historical personage represented.

The picture of King Henry is exceptionally good. He is spoken of as good, bookish, pious, weak, harmless, and all these adjectives are apt. There is no doubt that he was a weakling, the weakest king that sat on England's throne. Historians agree on that. He came at a time when affairs in England demanded a strong hand to control and a wise mind to judge, but he possessed neither of these; it is true that he assumed the throne while yet an infant, and that the government through his adolescent years was conducted by his uncles, but if he had possessed the traits of leadership he would have assimilated the principles of statesmanship to which he was exposed and would have emerged a great figure instead of the figurehead he became. He lacked the aggressiveness and energy of his father and grandfather, much preferring to study philosophy and the classics than statecraft. He was gentle and kindhearted, disliking heartily the quarreling and bickering that constantly was going on around him. He was deeply religious, and Shakespeare would have us believe that he would far rather retire into some monastery with his books than to be a participant in the embroglios characteristic of his time. Warrior he was not, to the great disgust of his wife who was a better soldier than he. Warwick calls him "faint

Henry" and "the easy melting king"; he says he could "wring
the awful sceptre from his fist, Were he as famous and as
bold in war As he is famed for mildness, peace, and prayer."
Clifford tells the King himself, "This too much lenity and
harmful piety must be laid aside." Henry replies, "I'll leave
my son my virtuous deeds behind, And would my father had
left me no more." Later the King thus soliloquizes:

> Would I were dead! If God's good will were so;
> For what is in this world but grief and woe?
> O God! methinks it were a happy life
> To be no better than a homely swain;
> To sit upon a hill, as I do now,
> To carve out dials quaintly, point by point,
> Thereby to see the minutes how they run,
> How many makes the hour full complete,
> How many hours brings about the day,
> How many days will finish up the year,
> How many years a mortal man may live.
> When this is known, then to divide the times;
> So many hours must I tend my flock,
> So many hours must I take my rest,
> So many hours must I contemplate,
> So many hours must I sport myself;
> So many days my ewes have been with young,
> So many weeks ere the poor fools will ean,
> So many years ere I shall shear the fleece.
> So minutes, hours, days, months, and years,
> Passed over to the end they were created,
> Would bring white hairs to a quiet grave.
> Ah, what a life were this! how sweet! how lovely!
> Gives not the hawthorn bush a sweeter shade
> To shepherds looking on their silly sheep,
> Than doth a rich embroidered canopy
> To kings that fear their subjects' treachery?

And Henry deposed is as gentle and content as when he wore
the crown:

> My crown is in my heart, not on my head;
> Not decked with diamonds and Indian stones,
> Nor to be seen. My crown is called content;
> A crown it is that seldom kings enjoy.

Weak and good and gentle and harmless as he was, he showed one last burst of spirit when Gloucester comes to the Tower to slay him. But when Richard plunges his dagger into the help- less king, Henry dies asking God to forgive his own sins and to pardon his murderer. Somehow, one cannot resist liking this unkingly king who was so out of place, so unfitted to hold the high office to which fate had elected him; and one wonders what might have been the result if the warlike Margaret had let him alone. No doubt his fate would have been different.

It is interesting to note the links that join this play with *Richard III,* which follows it chronologically. In scene VI of Act IV, King Henry calls young Henry Richmond to him and lays his hand on his head:

> Come hither, England's hope. If secret powers
> Suggest but truth to my divining thoughts,
> This pretty lad will prove our country's bliss.
> His looks are full of peaceful majesty,
> His head by nature framed to wear a crown,
> His hand to wield a sceptre, and himself
> Likely in time to bless a regal throne.

The best link of all, however, is the character of Richard of Gloucester. Cruel, deceitful, strong, deformed, he is introduced to us in the fifth act of *Henry VI, Part II;* but his first speech has a bite to it. When called upon by his father to be his surety when York is cornered by the Lancastrians, Edward replies, "Ay, noble father, if our words will serve." But Richard adds, "And if words will not, then our weapons shall." And in the same scene young Richard it is who slays the great Somerset; doing so, he utters a very characteristic line:

> Priests pray for enemies, but princes kill.

The *Second Part* ends with Salisbury's praise of Richard's prowess.

The *Third Part* is full of Richard of Gloucester. He fights valiantly throughout to establish his brother Edward's claim to the crown; he slays Clifford. But he knows his own limitations. He is ambitious, proud, but recognizes that the normal life of other men is not for him, because of his deformity. Of himself he speaks:

Well, say there is no kingdom then for Richard;
What other pleasure can the world afford?
I'll make my heaven in a lady's lap,
And deck my body in gay ornaments,
And witch sweet ladies with my words and looks!
O miserable thought! and more unlikely
Than to accomplish twenty golden crowns!
Why, love forswore me in my mother's womb;
And, for I should not deal in her soft laws,
She did corrupt frail nature with some bribe,
To shrink mine arm up like a withered shrub;
To make an envious mountain on my back,
Where sits deformity to mock my body;
In shape my legs of an unequal size;
To disproportion me in every part,
Like a chaos, or an unlicked bear-whelp
That carries no impression like the dam.
And am I then a man to be beloved?
O monstrous fault, to harbour such a thought!
Then, since this earth affords no joy to me,
But to command, to check, to o'er bear such
As are of better person than myself,
I'll make my heaven to dream upon the crown,
And, whiles I live, to account this world but hell,
Until my mis-shaped trunk that bears this head
Be round impaled with a glorious crown.
. . . .
And from that torment I will free myself,
Or hew my way out with a bloody axe.
Why, I can smile, and murder whiles I smile,
And cry "Content" to that which grieves my heart,
And wet my cheeks with artificial tears,
And frame my face to all occasions.
I'll drown more sailors than the mermaid shall;
I'll slay more gazers than the basilisk;
I'll play the orator as well as Nestor,
Deceive more slily than Ulysses could,
And, like a Sinon, take another Troy.
I can add colours to the chameleon,
Change shapes with Proteus for advantages,
And set the murderous Machiavel to school.
Can I do this, and cannot get a crown?
Tut, were it farther off, I'll pluck it down.

But the best characterisation of Richard is found in Henry's last speech, when he addresses Richard, who has come to the Tower to murder the ex-king.

> The owl shrieked at thy birth, an evil sign;
> The night-crow cried, aboding luckless time;
> Dogs howled, and hideous tempest shook down trees;
> The raven rooked her on the chimney top;
> And chattering pies in dismal discord sung.
> Thy mother felt more than a mother's pain,
> And yet brought forth less than a mother's hope,
> To wit, an indigested and deformed lump,
> Not like the fruit of such a goodly tree.
> Teeth hadst thou in thy head when thou wast born,
> To signify thou cam'st to bite the world.

Richard could abide no more of such, and stabbed the hapless deposed monarch. But in his heart he knew that most of what Henry had said was true. After Henry dies, Richard continues:

> For I have often heard my mother say
> I came into the world with my legs forward.
> Had I not reason, think ye to make hast
> And seek their ruin that usurped our right?
> The midwife wondered and the women cried,
> "O, Jesus bless us, he is born with teeth!"
> And so I was; which plainly signified
> That I should snarl and bite and play the dog.
> Then, since the heavens have shaped my body so,
> Let hell make crooked my mind to answer it.
> I have no brother, I am like no brother;
> And this word, "love," which greybeards call divine,
> Be resident in men like one another,
> But not in me. I am myself alone.

"I am myself alone." No other four words in the English language could so well describe Richard of Gloucester. From this moment to the time when Richard himself occupied the lofty eminence of the English throne, he went his lone way. Many there were who thought they were close to the great duke, but they soon found out their mistake. Buckingham, whom Richard called "my other self", whom Richard used as a stepping

THE HOUSE OF TUDOR

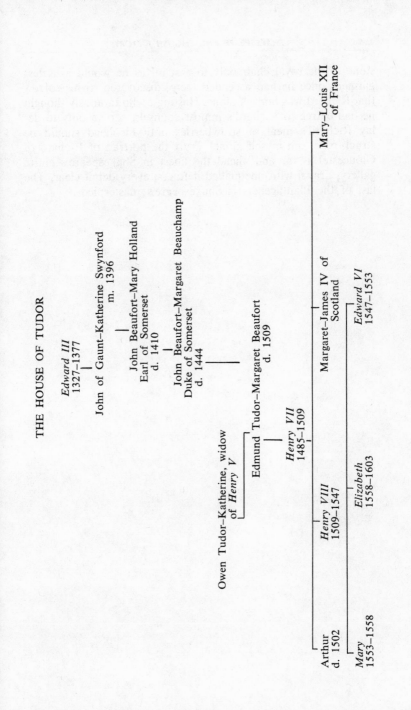

Edward III
1327–1377

John of Gaunt–Katherine Swynford
m. 1396

John Beaufort–Mary Holland
Earl of Somerset
d. 1410

John Beaufort–Margaret Beauchamp
Duke of Somerset
d. 1444

Owen Tudor–Katherine, widow
of *Henry V*

Edmund Tudor–Margaret Beaufort
d. 1509

Henry VII
1485–1509

Henry VIII
1509–1547

Margaret–James IV of
Scotland

Mary–Louis XII
of France

Arthur
d. 1502

Mary
1553–1558

Elizabeth
1558–1603

Edward VI
1547–1553

stone to the royal chair only to cast off as he would a useless garment once he had ascended there, discovered to his sorrow that Richard was himself alone. Hastings, who fatuously thought he had entrée to Richard's inmost counsels, served only to delay Richard's meal of strawberries until his head should be struck off. I am myself alone! Truly the portrait of Richard of Gloucester is far and ahead the finest in Shakespeare's entire gallery, drawn with unequalled deftness, every detail clear. The last of the Plantagenets is Shakespeare's masterpiece.

CHAPTER IX

Edward IV - Richard III

Edward IV: 1461-1483   Richard III: 1483-1485

Born 1441; married 1464   Born 1452; married, 1473
Elizabeth Woodville   Anne Neville

Kings of France: Louis XI (d. 1483); Charles VIII.

The first ten years of Edward's reign, the most troublous
period of his experiences, have been covered in the preceding
chapter. He was at times king, and at times he was fleeing from
the wrath of Margaret and Warwick, leaving his throne to be
occupied by the puppet Henry. The battle of Tewkesbury, however, in 1471, brought an end to the Wars of the Roses,
and at the same time established Edward once and for all on
the throne, and thenceforward most of his troubles were over.
In 1475 he found himself so strongly entrenched that he decided to make an expedition into France in order to settle
matters which had so long been in a state of upset in that country. Louis, however, was too keen a strategist to allow himself
to come into direct contact with the English forces; by a series
of diplomatic maneuvers he brought it about that Edward became willing to discuss terms. The two kings met on the bridge
in the town of Picquigny on the Somme, where a truce was
agreed on to last seven years; Louis was to pay Edward 75,000
crowns in cash and a pension of 50,000 crowns a year; Edward was to release Margaret of Anjou; and the Dauphin,
Charles, was to marry Edward's oldest daughter, Elizabeth. Thus
peace was established in France.

Back home again, Edward felt secure so far as political affairs were concerned; but in his own family he had cause for worry. In 1473 Richard of Gloucester had married Anne Neville, much against the will of Clarence, who had already married her sister, Isabel; Clarence was unwilling for his chances of coming into the wealth of the great Warwick, his father-in-law, to be thus divided in half. The result of this marriage was constant quarrels between the two brothers; and since Edward trusted Gloucester but had a justifiedly poor opinion of Clarence's honesty and fidelity, he had difficulty in preventing his brothers from coming to blows in the matter. Edward finally found a way to solve his problem. In 1478 in a meeting of parliament Edward personally charged his brother Clarence with treason, chiefly on the ground of Clarence's action in 1471. Both houses of parliament passed a bill of attainder against Clarence, and on it Clarence was put to death.

Very little of importance occurred in England during the remainder of Edward's reign. In April, 1483, after a short illness, Edward died. Surviving him were his two sons, Edward thirteen years old, and Richard, eleven, and his daughter, Elizabeth, 18.

Once again England now had a child-king. Experience had taught the English that no good could be expected from such a contingency, for their bitter experiments with Richard II and Henry VI had proven that when the government is in the hands of a protector almost any evil may be expected. It is small wonder, then, that the accession of so young a king excited more fear than hope in the nation, and paved the way for his dethronement. For the time had come when the common people could make and unmake kings.

Then too there was a very highly developed factionalism. While Edward IV was living, his strength and determined character kept down whatever discords might have existed at court, though the quarrels of Gloucester and Clarence more than once promised to cause an eruption of bitter feeling there. No sooner was Edward dead, however, than the struggle of the various parties to acquire power manifested itself, and the situation again became dangerous. There were the Woodvilles, raised into prominence and power by Edward to offset the strength of the Nevilles. Their leaders were the queen, her brothers, Anthony, Earl Rivers, and Richard and Edward Woodville, and her sons by her first marriage, Thomas Grey, Earl of

Dorset, and Sir Edward Grey. Then there were the lords of the council, chief of whom was Lord Hastings; not less potent was Thomas, Lord Stanley, who had married Margaret Beaufort, and Thomas Rotherham, Archbishop of York, and John Morton, Bishop of Ely. Beyond the official circle stood Henry Stafford, Duke of Buckingham, great-great-grandson of Thomas, Duke of Gloucester, son of Edward III. But looming more powerful than any of these was Richard of Gloucester, Edward's only surviving brother, a man of powerful personality and great reputation as a warrior and administrator.

No sooner was Edward IV dead than steps were taken by the Woodvilles to acquire control of the person of young Edward, the new king. The young prince was at his castle Ludlow at the time. Gloucester was on a military expedition in Yorkshire; Buckingham was at home on his estate; the queen and her family were in London. The council passed a ruling that the Woodvilles should not send an escort of more than two thousand to conduct young Edward to London to be crowned. Gloucester was on his way south, and on April 29, 1483, found himself within ten miles of the young king and his escort. Gloucester and Buckingham met, and they decided the best method of evading the power of the Woodvilles was to take action before they got into their stronghold, London. Thereupon they seized Rivers and Grey, who were leading the party of escort, and sent them under arrest to the north, while they themselves appointed themselves as escort to the young prince. Before they reached London news of the arrest of Grey and Rivers preceded them, and the queen with her other children took sanctuary at Westminster. When the party reached London, Hastings and the council declared Gloucester protector, and the Woodvilles were thus completely routed.

Richard entered upon his duties as protector on May 4, 1483. Plans were made for the coronation of the young king on June 22. But Gloucester had some plans of his own. On June 13, at a meeting of the council in the Tower of London, Richard accused Hastings of having plotted with the Woodvilles; he demanded the immediate execution of that unhappy lord. Gloucester next had Dr. Shaw, brother of the lord-mayor of London, to preach a sermon at St. Paul's Cross in which he insisted that Edward Fourth's marriage with Elizabeth Woodville

was illegal because of a pre-contract to Lady Eleanor But-
ler; that the children of Clarence had no right in the succession
because of their father's attainder; and that the only true right
to the crown now lay in Richard of Gloucester. On June 17 a
group of nobles and citizens waited on Richard, asking him to
accept the crown; with some show of hesitation he consented.
Rivers and Grey were put to death at Pontefract Castle. On
June 26 Richard declared himself king.

The reign of the uncrowned young king Edward V is reck-
oned to have come to an end on June 25. Young Edward, with
his brother Richard, had disappeared from view immediately
upon his deposition, and now the rumour spread that the two
had been secretly put to death within the walls of the Tower.
No details were known for twenty years; in 1502 Sir James
Tyrrel confessed that he had been employed to strangle the
young princes and to dispose of their bodies within the Tower.
In 1674 the skeletons of two children were discovered under an
old stair in the Tower.

A conspiracy against Richard III now was formed by John
Morton, Bishop of Ely, and Buckingham, the purpose of which
was to restore young Edward V to the throne. However, when
his death was ascertained, the conspirators turned their attention toward the only surviving Yorkist, Elizabeth, sister of the
young princes. Their plan was that she should marry young
Henry Tudor, now an exile in France. Negotiations were opened
with Margaret Beaufort, mother of Henry Tudor, and with
Elizabeth, the queen-dowager, looking toward the consummation of this arrangement. The plan was acceptable, and preparations went forward. Henry organized forces in France, and
Buckingham and Morton were to join him as he landed on October 18, 1483. A storm, however, wrecked the entire plan;
Henry's fleet was dispersed, and Buckingham was left unpro-
tected; Buckingham's men soon deserted him, he was taken,
and immediately put to death for treason. Henry returned
safely to Brittany.

Richmond determined to make further and more careful preparations for an invasion of England. Richard, too, realising
the power of his adversary, went about preparing for the inevitable conflict. In 1484 Richard somehow managed to come
to terms with Elizabeth, the queen-mother, that he should marry

young Elizabeth at the death of Anne. Anne conveniently died in 1485. Richard, however, was told by his advisers that a marriage with his own niece would outrage the feelings of the whole country, and he assured them he would discard any such plan. Henry sailed from Harfleur on August 1, 1485, and landed at Milford Haven on the 7th. He started out toward London, and as he went his forces became augmented.

On August 22, 1485, the two armies made contact at Bosworth. A fierce battle ensued. Richard fought bravely but the odds were against him, and finally he fell in the thick of the fighting, pierced with many wounds. The crown which he had worn during the battle was picked up by Sir William Stanley and placed on the head of Henry Tudor, Earl of Richmond.

Henry marched to London, entered the city on September 3, and on November 7 he was formally crowned king as Henry VII. In January, 1486, he married Elizabeth of York; this union of the houses of York and Lancaster brought to an end the struggle of the Wars of the Roses, a struggle that had torn England with bloody fratricide for sixty years.

King Richard III
The Play

Historic Time: 1471-1485.
Dramatic Time: 11 days.
Place: England.
Purpose: To show the ruin of ideal villainy.
Date of Composition: 1593

The *Chronicles* of Holinshed continue to be the source of most of Shakespeare's material for the historical plays; *Richard III* is no exception. The outlines of the characters furnished by Holinshed, however, are in every case filled in by Shakespeare, whose imagination caught up and vitalized the men and women who are hinted at by the historian. As in the other plays, Shakespeare has taken the mere historical skeleton and equipped it with flesh and blood and nerves and brain; the speeches of his characters are Shakespeare's own, and the vital touch which the historian misses the genius of the master playwright has instilled into every person who walks across his stage. Richard may not have been the diabolical villain the poet pictures to us, but history has not yet disproved it. Until it does we stand and wonder at the reality of Shakespeare's Richard.

The play begins with Richard endeavoring to explain to himself the reason for his villainy. Richard has offtimes been compared to Iago; however much alike they may be, there is this fundamental difference between them: you can never believe Iago even when he is speaking in soliloquies, but Richard speaks the truth when no one is listening. The greatest hypocrite in literature, he is himself only when alone, but he is himself then. Since then Richard is determined to prove a villain, he goes on to tell us what his immediate plans are, thus introducing the action that is to follow. He has gotten King Edward wrought up over a prophecy that his house is to come to ruin through some person whose name begins with the letter *G*, Gloucester has whispered to Edward that naturally George, Duke of Clarence, starts his name with G; and Clarence is immediately put in prison for safe-keeping. But as Richard meets Clarence on his way to the Tower under escort of a guard, Gloucester becomes immediately the oily, sympathetic brother, suggesting by word and innuendo that the Woodvilles are behind this latest move against the king's family.

Then comes one of the most remarkable scenes in all drama. Richard meets Anne Neville, following the corpse of her father-in-law, the murdered Henry, to his interment. He stops the procession and sets out to woo her, the lady whose husband and father-in-law he himself had slain. And Shakespeare would have us believe that Anne capitulated as he describes it. Some critics have seen in this Shakespeare's dig at womankind in general; they say that the poet has suffered at the hands of woman and thus expressed his opinion of the whole sex. The more logical explanation is that Shakespeare's reason was that of dramatic economy. He incorporated into one scene what required historically two years, for Henry VI was murdered in 1471 and Richard married Anne in 1473. But also there is a better reason for the poet's treatment of the courtship scene as he did. In no subtler way could he portray Richard's powerful personality than by having him take Anne in her moment of most intense hate and winning from her her consent to be his wife. Richard was by far the most important personage in the kingdom, the man with the most power and influence, and it was actually a tremendous compliment to Anne that he should thus offer her marriage. Disregarding his personal unattractiveness, his ✕ personality and his influence were enough to turn the head of any woman in the kingdom, and Anne is not so much to be blamed for her action in the matter. But Richard confesses he does not love her. He is marrying her for one reason only; to get for himself Anne's share in the vast Warwick estates; once in possession, he is through with Anne, and will quickly rid himself of her. But Richard is as surprised at the success of his courtship as we are, for he says satirically:

> My dukedom to a beggarly denier
> I do mistake my person all this while.
> Upon my life, she finds, though I cannot,
> Myself to be a marvellous proper man.
> I'll be at charges for a looking-glass,
> And entertain a score or two of tailors,
> To study fashions to adorn my body.
> Since I am crept in favor with myself,
> I will maintain it with some little cost.

We learn next that King Edward is ill, preparing us, of course for his immediate death. Queen Elizabeth and her brother and son are conversing with Buckingham and Derby, when Gloucester joins them. His coming is a signal for a general wrangle, emphasizing the bitterness existing between the Woodvilles and Gloucester. While they upbraid one another, Queen Margaret enters unobserved by any one on the stage, and remains unseen for quite a while while she listens to their recriminations. The appearance of Margaret here is of course unhistorical, perhaps the farthest Shakespeare had deviated from actuality throughout the entire play. After the Peace of Picquigny, in 1475, Margaret returned to her home in France, never again to visit England. Shakespeare introduces her here, however, very effectively, for she seems more of a spirit than real flesh and blood; she comes and goes unseen, passes among those in the play with no one to notice, comes forward to utter her bitter curses, withdraws whither no one seems to know, and appears only once again, when she returns to gloat over the consummation of her prophecies. Though she actually appears on the scene but twice in the entire play, her spirit broods over the whole action; and each victim of Richard dying remembers Margaret's curse and admits its justice. She represents Nemesis, the spirit of vengeance. Shakespeare makes of her a very effective character in the drama.

The scene depicting the murder of Clarence contains some of the best poetry of the play. The horror of the murder's being committed on the stage is somewhat softened by three elements of relief: the beauty of the poetry, the fact that one of the murderers relents, and the knowledge the reader has of Clarence's guilt.

Act II is introduced by a scene in which King Edward, realising that his end is near, undertakes to patch up the differences among those of his court. We learn that Clarence is dead by an order of the king which reached the executioner earlier than a later order rescinding the first. Apparently the queen recognizes Gloucester's hand in the matter. Then Shakespeare introduces a symbolic scene where Edward is forced to grant leniency to a servant of Derby's who had slain a gentleman; this gives the king opportunity to upbraid himself and those of his counsellors for not having been lenient with Clarence.

In the next scene King Edward is dead. Plans are being made that young Edward be escorted from Ludlow to London for his coronation. Buckingham and Gloucester determine that they will see to it that the prince shall lose the escort of the Woodvilles on the way up. The two dukes go to meet the prince, and Rivers, Grey, and Vaughan are arrested and sent to Pomfret Castle, a place that never yet boded anyone any good. In the meantime, word of this action reaching the queen, she takes her children and seeks sanctuary.

Act III begins with the arrival of young Edward in London, only to find his mother and younger brother absent in sanctuary. Hastings is sent to summon them, but they refuse to leave the church. Buckingham dispatches Cardinal Bourchier and Hastings to fetch young York, saying that there was no sanctuary where there was no danger; therefore to bring the boy and his mother by force would not be a violation of sanctuary. But Elizabeth knew Gloucester and Buckingham better than they thought. However, the messengers succeeded in getting the other prince, and the two brothers are sent to the Tower for "safe keeping."

Gloucester's next step is to sound Hastings, to find how he stood in regard to Edward's being removed from the succession. In the meantime Rivers, Grey, and Vaughan are executed at Pomfret, each remembering poignantly Margaret's prophecy concerning them. Next comes the famous "strawberry scene." The Council assemble at the Tower for dinner. They discuss the date of coronation of Edward, and decide that the following day would be propitious, but hesitate to pass on it until Gloucester should arrive. He comes, excusing himself for oversleeping, and immediately sends the Bishop of Ely for some strawberries for his lunch. Hastings fatuously thinks he is one of Gloucester's favorites, thinks he knows Gloucester's inmost secrets and all his habits. But Buckingham and Gloucester have gone out to discuss methods of catching Hastings unawares. They return, and Richard, scowling, demands what punishment those deserve who are guilty of prevailing upon his body with witchcraft, at the same time lifting his sleeve and revealing an arm that had been withered since birth. Hastings makes the mistake of talking too much, and walked into the trap laid for him. Richard then gave orders for the removal of Hastings' head, saying he would not eat until he saw his order carried out. Thus Hastings stayed dinner in the Tower. He too remembered Margaret's curse as he was led away to his death.

The next thing to be done, of course, was to justify the order for the execution of Hastings, and Gloucester and Buckingham took immediate steps. Scene five has these stage directions: "Enter Gloucester and Buckingham, in rotten armor, marvellous ill-favoured." Shakespeare very subtly tells us here that the two conspirators, pretending to be in great danger from their enemies (Hastings and others) had snatched up old armor that neither would have deigned to put on otherwise, but were glad to have any kind of armor in the present emergency. They pretend great fear, looking over the shoulder as if expecting an onslaught at any moment, all for the benefit of the lord-mayor and citizens who now appear. They then explain that Hastings, whose head is now brought in, had been caught in a conspiracy against the state, and had thus been executed peremptorily. In all the reaches of literature there is no hypocrite to equal Shakespeare's Richard.

Gloucester sends Buckingham to arrange for a speech in the

Guildhall declaring Edward's marriage to Elizabeth illegitimate, and he dispatches Lovell to Dr. Shaw to procure the same end.

The next scene has two purposes: to give Buckingham time to make his speech at the Guildhall and report his results; and to prove by the words of the scrivener that Hastings had been doomed long before he had been arrested.

Buckingham's speech at the Guildhall was not so satisfactory. He received scarcely any applause, but fortunately his own followers had been coached to applaud vigorously, and Buckingham, bowing to the crowd, said, "Thanks, gentle citizens and friends; this general applause and cheerful shout argues your wisdom and your love to Richard." One is reminded of the *claquers* opera singers frequently employ, who, seated at strategic places throughout the house, clap vigorously at just the right moment, knowing that if one person begins clapping in a full house, the crowd will begin doing so too.

The last scene in Act III is a masterpiece. Here is the crowning brazenness of the arch-hypocrite, who dares to decline the offer of the crown he has struggled for so long, who hesitates only to have the crown forced on him by his admirers. Just so, a poker player holding four aces passes in order to be able to raise. Imagine Richard, entering above between two priests, with a prayer-book in his hand, his eyes raised piously to heaven! And Buckingham is just the man to prod the citizens on, to make them do what the two would have them do. No, Gloucester cannot accept the offer of the crown, for it would take him away from his worship. He is surprised that the citizens do not recognize that he is too busy with his religion to be bothered with being king. They will have to find someone else. And he reproves Buckingham who dares to swear in his pious presence! Such consummate hypocrisy has never been more adroitly presented. Finally Richard, after much urging, is led to reconsider, and yields to the importunity of his admirers. So with "Long live King Richard!" we come to the climax of the action of the play.

Soon we see Richard crowned. Noteworthy is the fact that when he ascends the throne he asks Buckingham to give him his hand—an extremely symbolic gesture. Buckingham throughout has been Richard's stepping-stone to the throne of England, his ladder whereby to mount the royal eminence. But such is

Richard's character, so much was he himself alone, that once he has climbed where he wishes to be, he throws down his ladder. He has no further use for it. Thus the stage is set for the quick end of Buckingham. Now crowned, Richard will not rest secure until the young princes are out of the way, and he wants Buckingham to see to it. But Buckingham shrinks from child murder. He asks for time to consider the royal order. Meantime Richard is seen to gnaw his underlip, an ominous sign. He gives orders for rumours to be spread that Anne is sick, so that her early demise will be accepted as natural. He is through with Anne as he is through with Buckingham. He must now marry his brother's daughter, the young Elizabeth, in order to strengthen his claim to the throne. Therefore Anne must be gotten rid of. He himself employs two murderers to kill the two princes in the Tower, no longer trusting Buckingham, and when Buckingham returns, he does not even ask him for an answer. When Buckingham requests the emoluments Richard had promised him, the king absolutely ignores him. The duke recognizes the handwriting on the wall, and resolves to get away immediately.

The murder scene which follows is relieved by the beauty of the poetry and the relenting of the murderers. We learn also that besides the princes, Richard has put Clarence's children where they will not worry him, that Anne is dead, and that his next move is to marry young Elizabeth. And news comes that Richmond is on the way.

Once more Margaret, she-wolf of France, returns, this time to gloat over the consummation of her curses and evil prophecies. Whence she comes we do not know, nor whither she goes. But she comes and goes like a wraith, as if the poet were trying to dramatize the influence of the absent ex-queen, to personify an influence that brooded over all the events of this troubled time, even though bodily she was absent many leagues in France. Not easily could the persons of this drama forget the dominating queen of Henry VI.

The scene in which Richard woos Elizabeth, the mother, for Elizabeth, the daughter, is almost as strange as that in which he persuaded Anne; perhaps more strange, for the demand was more unnatural. And Elizabeth, the mother, appears to yield; we know, however, that she was merely working for time, for she

knew how utterly useless it was for her to refuse Richard anything he wanted outright. He was a man who took what he
wanted. So she seems to accede to his request. But news comes
that even now Richmond is landing in England, and we know
that Richard's days are numbered. Margaret is the Nemesis,
Buckingham the steppingstone, but Richmond is the Minister of
Chastisement, and he is on his way.

Events occur now with increasing rapidity. Buckingham, making an effort to join Henry Tudor, meets disaster and is taken.
He is executed for treason, as all others would be, if Richard
could get at them. Buckingham too remembers Margaret's
prophecy concerning him. Richmond and Richard meet on Bosworth Field. Their tents are pitched side by side on the stage.
The ghosts of Richard's victims, one by one in the order they
met death, appear and enter first the tent of the sleeping Richard to trouble him, and then the tent of Richmond, to encourage
him. Richard wakes from his dream calling for a horse, prophecy of his famous cry in battle the following day. Each of the
leaders rise early and addresses his troops. The battle begins.
Richard, fighting bravely with his back to the wall, is finally
slain by Henry; you are forced to admire the courage of the man
who is more noble in his death than he ever was in his whole
life. Somehow he redeems himself, not by dying, but by the
manner in which he died.

At last the roses, white and red, are joined, and the sixty
years of war are over. Affairs in England for a time look bright.

More than any other play Shakespeare wrote, *Richard III*
is a one-man play. All the action of the drama, all the characters are subordinated to the action and character of the ambitious duke. In this respect, at least, Shakespeare shows the
influence of Christopher Marlowe, who had written his four
great one-man plays before Shakespeare even began his dramatic career. Of course *Hamlet* is a one-man play; often has
the question been asked, What would *Hamlet* be with Hamlet
left out? The same question could be applied to *Richard III*.
Richard dominates every scene of the play; his ambition and
cruelty is the spring of all the action in the drama; he is the
unifying character. Around his personality is built the development of the entire plot; truly is it a portrayal of the rise and fall
of Richard of Gloucester.

Shakespeare followed Holinshed very closely, seizing with his imagination even the merest hints in the historical narrative, and making of them a realistic portrait of the times. Of the death, for instance, of Clarence, Holinshed says:

Finallie, the duke of Clarence was cast into the Tower, and therewith adiudged for a traiter, and priuilie drowned in a butt of malmesie, the eleuenth of March, in the beginning of the seuenteenth yeare of the king's reigne.

Although king Edward were consenting to Clarence's death, yet he much did both lament his infortunate chance, & repent his sudden execution: insomuch that when anie person sued to him for the pardon of malefactors condemned to death, he would accustomablie saie, & openlie speake: "Oh infortunate brother, for whose life not one would make sute!"

Almost bodily did Shakespeare employ Holinshed's narrative of the strawberry scene:

Manie lords assembled in the Tower, and there sat in councell, deuising the honourable solemnitie of the kings coronation; of which the time appointed then so neere approached, that the pageants and subtilties were in making daie & night at Westminster, and much vittels killed therfore, that afterward was cast awaie. These lords so sitting togither communing of this matter, the protector came in amongst them, first about nine of the clocke, saluting them courteouslie, and excusing himselfe that he had been from them so long; saieng merilie that he had beene a sleeper that daie.

After a little talking with them, he said vnto the bishop of Elie: "My lord, you haue verie good strawberries at your garden in Holborn, I require you let us haue a messe of them" "Gladlie, my lord," (quoth he) "would God I had some beeter thing as readie to your pleasure as that!" And therewithal in all the hast he sent his seruent for a messe of strawberries. The protector set the lords fast in communing, & thereupon, praieng them to spare him for a little while, departed thense. And soone after one houre, betweene ten and eleuen, he returned into the chamber amongst them, all changed, with a woonderfull soure angrie countenance, knitting the browes, frowning, and fretting and gnawing on his lips: and so sat him downe in his place.

All the lords were much dismaid, and sore maruelled at this maner of change, and what thing should him aile.

Then, when he had sitten still a while, thus he began: "What were they worthie to haue that compasse and imagine the destruction of me, being so neere of bloud vnto the king, and protector of his roiall person and his realmne?" At this question, all the lords sat sore astonied, musing much by whome this question should be meant, of which euerie man wist himself cleere. Then the lord chamberlaine (as he that for the loue betweene them thought he might be boldest with him) answered and said, that they were worthie to be punished as heinous traitors, whatsoeuer they were. And all the other affirmed the same. "That is" (quoth he) "yonder sorceresse my brothers wife, and other with hir" (meaning the queene).

At these words manie of the other lords were greatlie abashed, that fauored hir. But the lord Hastings was in his mind better content, that it was mooved by hir, than by anie other whome he loued better: albeit his heart somewhat grudged, that he was not afore made of councell in this matter, as he was of the taking of her kinred, and of their putting to death, which were by his assent before deuised to be beheaded at Pomfret this selfe same dait; in which he was not ware that it was by other deuised that he himselfe should be beheaded the same daie at London. Then said the protector: "Ye shall all see in what wise that sorceresse, and that other witch of hir councell, Shores wife, with their affinitie, haue, by their sorcerie and witchcraft, wasted my bodie." And therwith he plucked vp his dublet sleeue to his elbow, vpon his left arme, where he shewed a weerish withered arme, and small; as it was neuer other.

Herevpon euerie mans mind sore misgave him, well perceiuing that this matter was but a quarell. For they well wist that the queene was too wise to go about anie such follie. And also, if she would, yet would she, of all folke least, make Shores wife of hir counsell; whome of all women she most hated, as that concubine whome the king hir husband had most loued. And also, no man was there present, but well knew that his arme was euer thus since his birth. Naithlesse, the lord chamberlain (which from the death of King Edward kept Shores wife, on whome he somewhat doted in the kings life, sauing, as it is said, he that while forbare hir of reverence toward the king, or else of a certain kind of fidelitie to his friend) answered and said: "Certeinlie, my lord, if they have so heinouslie doone, they be worthie heinous punishment."

"What" (quoth the protector) "thou seruest me, I weene, with 'ifs' and with 'ands': I tell thee they haue so doone, and that I will make good on thy bodie, traitor!! and therewith, as in a great anger, he clapped his fist, upon the board a great rap. At which token, one cried "Treason!" without the chamber. Therewith a doore clapped, and in come there rushing men in harnesse, as manie as the chamber might hold. And anon the protector said to Hastings: "I arrest thee, traitor!" "What me, my lord?" (quoth he.) "yea, thee, traitor!" quoth the protector.

Then were they all quickelie bestowed in diuerse chambers, except the lord chamberlaine, whome the protector bad speed and shriue him apace, "for, by saint Paule" (quoth he) "I will not to dinner till I see thy head off!" It booted him not to ask whie, but heauilie he tooke a priest at aduenture, and made a short shrift for a longer would not be suffered, the protector made so much hast to dinner, which he might not go to, vntil this were doone, for sauing of his oth.

Of Richard's character the chronicler continues:

Richard, the third sonne, of whome we now intreat, was in wit and courage equall with either of them, in bodie and prowesse farre under them both; litle of stature, ill featured of limmes, crooke backed, his left shoulder much higher than his right, hard favoured of visage, and such as is in states called warlie, in other men otherwise; he was malicious, wrathful, enuious, and from afore his birth euer froward. It is for truth reported, that the duchesse, his mother, had so much adoo in hir trauell, that she could not be deliuered of him vncut; and that he came into the world with the feet forward, as men be borne outward, and (as the fame runneth also) not vntoothed.

Buckingham in this play was Henry, Duke of Buckingham, son of Humphrey, Earl of Stafford, killed at St. Albans in 1455, and great-grandson of Anne, daughter of Thomas, Duke of Gloucester, who was killed at Calais during the reign of Richard II. Buckingham therefore was great-great-great-grandson of Edward III, and had blood in his veins as royal as that of Richard III himself. He, like Richmond, was a Beaufort through his mother, and was heir of half the lands of the Bohuns.

The evil in Richard's character has quite obliterated any historical account of the good. As a matter of fact, once having become king, he seemed to have set out to rule wisely and to improve conditions in his kingdom, conditions that very much needed improvement. Strange as it may seem he undertook to promote justice throughout the nation and in every way possible to restore the rights of those who had been deprived. To many who had suffered loss of property under attainders under the Lancastrians Richard made restitution; and he made an effort thoroughly to purge courts of law of inequality and injustice. He took an especial interest in the extension of commerce and the encouragement of art; he gave special encouragement to the Universities of Oxford and Cambridge, and in other ways assisted the advancement of education in the realm. The new art of printing, recently introduced into England, received his protection and support; under his patronage the art of printing increased mightily, so that books, hitherto accessible only to the privileged classes, now came into the hands of all who felt the impulse to read. The king delighted in music, and did much to encourage the increased appreciation of music among his subjects. All in all, he was rather an unusual statesman, and accomplished much in statesmanship in the short period he occupied the throne. These facts are usually lost sight of when we contemplate the Richard of Shakespeare and Holinshed, the ambitious, selfish hypocrite who climbed to the throne over the bodies of his murdered kinsmen. But even the devil should have his due.

One final observation should be recorded here. Richard III became king of England with the support and will of the common people. It is a long step from the autocracy of King John— the king who could do no wrong—to the democratic Richard, who actually courted the commonalty, knowing that his very incumbency of the throne depended on their good will. Shakespeare paints vividly Richard's efforts to win the people to his side: Buckingham's speech in the Guildhall, Dr. Shaw's sermon in St. Paul's, and particularly the crowning scene of them all when the Lord Mayor and the *citizens* offer the crown to the hesitant duke as he stood between two priests with a prayerbook in his hand. Imagine Richard II doing that, or Edward III, his grandfather! But the time had arrived when the common people had come into their own, and Richard of Gloucester knew it. Shakespeare also knew it, and very ably presents it to us, and very dramatically. Thus we see in bold relief one of the themes running throughout the ten historical plays— the rise of the common people; linked inseparably with it, of course, is the easily apparent decline of feudalism. The Commons' quick acceptance of Richard may be easily explained, too. In the first place, they were chary of child kings; they had had too much experience with them, and knew that in practically every instance, they had come to grief when their king was a child. Richard II and Henry VI had proven to the common people that boy kings brought trouble, and they were not enthusiastic over young Edward V on that account. Therefore they did not ask many questions when he was quietly put out of the way. In the second place, Richard of Gloucester was by all odds the most powerful and influential man at that time in the kingdom, and he was admired and respected by the commons. He had proven his military ability and administrative leadership; they preferred to accept a known quantity rather than one unknown. No wonder they acquiesced so readily.

CHAPTER X

Henry VII, 1485-1509

Born 1456; married, 1486, Elizabeth of York.
King of France: Charles VIII, d. 1498; Louis XII, d. 1515.
King of Spain: Ferdinand and Isabella.

Henry Tudor assumed the position of king on the battle-field of Bosworth, and two weeks later entered London in royal state, on September 3, 1485. He arranged for his coronation on October 30, and summoned parliament to meet for that occasion. Richard III was declared to be a usurper and his supporters were declared traitors; however, Henry adopted a policy of leniency toward all who had been with Richard, and there were no executions to follow, as was usual in such cases. His attitude soon established confidence in him, and the next step was to consummate his marriage with Elizabeth, daughter of Edward the Fourth. This marriage took place in January, 1486.

Henry had three objects in mind. The first was to secure the throne for himself by removing all who might claim rivalry; however, he chose to do this more by diplomacy than by ruthlessness, for England had grown tired of the endless bloodshed that accompanied any change in dynasty. The second aim was to reduce the power of the nobility, and thus to increase the power of the throne. A third plan he undertook was to take an active part in European politics, and to do this he strengthened himself by various matrimonial alliances. The early years of Henry's reign, as might be expected, were full of uprisings and conspiracies to remove the king and to place one of the various surviving Yorkists on the throne. Henry had to deal with several of these conspiracies, among them a number seeking to effect their means by use of imposters. A boy named Simnel, who had been trained to impersonate young Edward Plantagenet, son of Clarence, became the focus of a rebellion, but the king easily suppressed that movement. In 1492 another imposter, Perkin Osbeck, who claimed to be young Richard, Duke of York, who had escaped from the Tower, appeared on the scene and fomented a rebellion which caused Henry considerable trouble before he fully put it down. After several years of effort, in which a number of plots were organized, Osbeck was finally defeated and hanged, but for a while, during the so-called Cornish Rebellion, he made considerable headway. However, after considerable difficulty, the king managed to suppress all attempts to dislodge him, and he was then able to turn his attention to his second great purpose, the curtailing of the power of the nobles.

To attack the power of the nobility Henry had as his chief aid a man named John Morton, who had been created Archbishop of Canterbury. Morton was shrewd, hard, and determined. New courts of justice were organized to do away with the evils in the system that had existed for so long a time. The king was unwilling to exact heavy taxes from his subjects, knowing how unpopular taxes were; so he resorted to a different method for getting money with which to conduct his government. This method was called "benevolences". This was really a demand on those who were wealthy, for money, with the exemption of those who were poor. However, this method had its weaknesses, and great injustice resulted from it. The system gave rise to the phrase "Morton's Fork", because Cardinal Morton gave instructions to the collectors "That if they met any who were sparing, they must tell them they must needs have, because they laid up; and if they were spenders they must needs have, because it was seen in their port and their manner of living." By this ingenious manner no man could escape. Henry grew rich as a result of his campaign, and at his death he left property, chiefly jewels, worth 18,000,000 pounds sterling.

Henry next turned his attention to foreign affairs. A European League had been formed against France, and Henry's participation was urged. Henry finally agreed to enter the League, and arrangements were made for the marriage of Henry's son,

Arthur, with Katharine of Aragon, daughter of Ferdinand and Isabella, of Spain. The marriage took place in 1501, but young Arthur died in April of the next year. Henry immediately made negotiations for Katherine's marriage to his next son, Henry, who had been born in 1491. The king also arranged for the marriage of his elder daughter, Margaret, to James IV, king of Scotland. Thus by marriage of his children to various foreign princes Henry sought to strengthen his power abroad.

Elizabeth, the queen, died in 1503. For six years there was much talk of Henry's marrying again to connect himself thereby with the great alliance, but nothing came of it. In 1509 the king died, leaving the kingdom in perhaps a better condition than it had been for a hundred years. Strong within and without, England was on the eve of a great awakening, not, however, fully to be realized until the days of Elizabeth, fifty years later. In many respects the reign of the Tudors was the most beneficial period of all English history. The Renaissance Movement was just reaching England; and with the discovery of America in 1492, immense strides were made in geographical discovery. In the reign of Henry VII the first European vessel ever to reach the mainland of North America was a British ship commanded by John Cabot. Great things were adoing. The period of the Middle Ages was over; the Modern Age began with Henry Tudor.

CHAPTER XI

Henry VIII, 1509-1547

Born 1491; married

1509, Katharine of Aragon, divorced 1533, d. 1536
1532, Anne Boleyn, executed 1536
1536, Jane Seymour, died 1537
1540, Anne of Cleves, divorced 1540, died 1557
1540, Katharine Howard, executed 1542
1543, Katharine Parr

Kings of France: Louis XII, d. 1515; Francis I, d. 1547.
Kings of Scotland: James IV, d. 1513; James V, d. 1542; Mary, deposed 1567.
King of Spain: Charles I, d. 1556.

Henry VIII has always been one of the most well-known monarchs of the English line, chiefly perhaps because of the popularity of his marital experiments. Usually when the uxorious king is mentioned, his name is greeted with a knowing smile. Of late there have been published several excellent biographies of the jovial monarch, and these tend to publicize the doings of the second Tudor. He was eighteen years of age when he acceded to the throne, and from the beginning showed himself as determined to be king as his father had done. He received his own ambassadors, conducted his own business, handled his own affairs, and generally showed great energy and judgment. His wit was quick and his manner was easy, so that he gained a popularity with his subjects that lasted throughout his life. He was fond of the lime-light and suffered no other to be the center of attention when he was present.

One of his first acts as king was to marry himself to his brother's widow, Katharine of Aragon. She was six years his senior, a woman of attractive personality, though not beautiful. She danced well, was a good musician, knew English perfectly, and was devoted to Henry.

The greatest man in the kingdom at this time was Thomas Wolsey, perhaps the foremost ecclesiastic England ever produced. He was born in 1471, son of a wealthy burgher, and was given the best education money could buy. He entered Oxford very young and received his bachelor of arts degree at the age of fifteen; he became fellow and bursar of Magdalen College. In 1506 he became royal chaplain to Henry VII; when Henry VIII became king the young monarch liked the bright energy of Wolsey and his advancement was rapid.

An invasion of France was indicated and Sir Edward Howard attacked the French fleet, defeated them, and opened up a passage to Calais, so that Henry and Wolsey soon were able to attack Tournai with success. But while Henry was in France James IV of Scotland, forgetting his alliance with Henry VII, decided to invade England with a large army. Queen Katharine had been left in charge in England, and she threw herself into the conflict with energy, organizing defense and stirring up enthusiasm.

The English forces were led by the Earl of Surrey, and they met the Scotch at Flodden Field, on the boundary between England and Scotland, on September 4, 1513. The English were victorious, James himself being slain on the field of battle; James's body, found in a heap of slain, was identified, and his blood-stained plaid was sent by Katharine as a trophy to her husband. This battle served more than as just one additional victory; it showed Europe that England could not be intimidated by an attack on her borders, and it served to render Scotland harmless for many years to come.

Meantime, in France, Henry had decided he did not care to continue war with that country, and he delegated to Wolsey the duty of arranging peace. With great secrecy negotiations were opened with France. It was arranged that Henry's sister, Mary Tudor, a beautiful girl of seventeen, should marry Louis XII, now fifty-two years old, and the terms were agreed upon. For a while this marriage accomplished its purpose of cementing friendship with France, but in 1515 Louis died. Naturally, this brought that alliance to an end, and Mary then married Charles Brandon, Duke of Suffolk. She thus became the grandmother of Lady Jane Grey, who caused Queen Elizabeth so much anxiety in later years.

Wolsey received promotion after promotion. In 1514 he became Bishop of Lincoln, and in 1515 Archbishop of York. At the same time Wolsey became Chancellor of England. In 1517 Henry found himself of sufficient influence to cause Pope Leo X to raise Wolsey to the Cardinalate, and to have him appointed papal legate to England. Immediately Wolsey began putting in operation his ideas concerning schools throughout the land, dissolving monasteries and making them into schools preparing for the universities. He also established a college at Oxford, called it Cardinal College, later changing it to Christ Church. Wolsey's ultimate ambition was to become Pope, but he was kept so busy with his secular duties that he was never able to realize his desire.

And now came Wolsey's great diplomatic opportunity. The new king of France, Francis I, was ambitious and energetic. He had penetrated into Italy and won tremendous prestige by his victories there. His influence came to be something to be feared in Europe, with the result that a coalition was again formed against France by the other European powers. Spain, Sicily, Naples, and the Netherlands, together with Austria and Germany decided it was to their interest to combine against the French; Wolsey considered it was therefore advantageous for England to form another alliance with the French in order to establish more or less a balance of power. Therefore it was arranged that Henry's only daughter, Mary, should marry the infant Dauphin and that Tournai should be restored to France for a consideration of the payment of 600,000 crowns. The pope, the emperor of Germany, and the king of Spain all agreed that peace was the better policy, and England, guided by Wolsey, appeared as the promoter of this peace project. In the meantime, the "Emperor of the Holy Roman Empire", Maximilian, died, and Charles of Spain was elected to succeed him. Wolsey now had to deal diplomatically with two powers, Charles and Francis. He decided upon a policy of neutrality and maintained friendship with both of them. Charles paid a visit to Henry, after which Henry crossed to Calais and held a conference with Francis in such formal state that the site of their interview has been designated as the "Field of the Cloth of Gold". On Henry's return, at Calais, he again interviewed Charles; thus England had the honor of having the two most powerful monarchs of Europe vieing with each other to win the friendship of Henry. The Field of the Cloth of Gold is considered a diplomatic triumph for Wolsey.

But another problem soon faced the brilliant cardinal. Henry and Katharine had been married eighteen years, but all their sons and daughters had died in infancy except Mary, a delicate girl, who had been affianced to the Duke of Orleans. Always the succession to the throne was a matter of paramount importance to the incumbent. If Henry VIII should die without children, the crown would go, first, to Margaret's son, James of Scotland, and next to her daughter; great fear was entertained that neither of these would be acceptable to the English people. The children of the other sister, Mary, were all girls. And now Henry developed a passion for a young lady of the court, Anne Boleyn, whom he earnestly desired to marry; to do so, a divorce with Katharine was necessary. Henry put the matter up to Wolsey.

The situation was aggravated by Katherine's connection with the Spanish royalty. Charles, the present emperor, was her nephew, and that monarch might easily take offense at any slight placed upon Katharine; therefore, the pope was unwilling to take any favorable stand concerning Henry's divorce, much as he desired to maintain Henry's friendship; the pope was between two fires. Various embassies were sent to the pope in an effort to get him to allow the case to be tried in Wolsey's court in England; but Pope Clement refused to submit to pressure, and in 1528 sent over Cardinal Campeggio to act as Wolsey's colleague. Delay after delay followed; Katharine appealed to Rome. At the same time, the impetuous and ardent Henry became more and more angry at the slowness of the affair, and he vented his anger on Wolsey, who was not in the least responsible for the delays. In 1529 Henry directed his attorney to sue for a writ against Wolsey; since Wolsey held his position through Henry, it followed that he could lose it the same way, and Wolsey knew it. Wolsey therefore signed a document acknowledging his wrong in acting as papal legate, and in every way knuckled to the king. By his obsequiousness Wolsey gained the king's pardon, but his two best servants, Stephen Gardiner and Thomas Cromwell, passed into the service of the king.

Wolsey's decline was rapid. On February 12, 1530, he received a full pardon from the king, but was forced to resign his bishoprics and to dwell away from the court. He lost caste completely. However, he kept up a correspondence with the French king through his physician, Dr. Augustine, who revealed all the letters to Wolsey's bitter enemy, the Duke of Norfolk, who immediately laid the matter before the king. Wolsey was arrested on November 4, 1530; he was being taken to London to stand trial for high treason when he died at Leicester Abbey on November 30. The fall of Wolsey marks one of the most important epochs in the reign of Henry VIII.

Wolsey was succeeded in the chancellorship by Sir Thomas More, one of the great scholars of his day. Educated at Oxford, he was a product of the Renaissance. He is perhaps best remembered today because of his *Utopia*, a Latin work in two parts, the first devoted to exposing the evils of the times, the second to a description of an ideal commonwealth. But he was an excellent lawyer and somewhat of a politician. He soon made himself conspicuous by his attacks on Wolsey, actions in very bad taste and destined to reveal his true character.

To press his divorce Henry now determined to summon parliament to meet on November 3, 1529. The divorce question did not seem to approach solution, however, and matters went along thus for several years. In 1532 More, who had become disgusted with the trend of affairs and particularly with Henry's divorce proceedings, resigned the chancellorship. Henry persisted in his efforts, endeavoring to persuade the pope to grant him a decree, but the pope was adamant. Then a new plan presented itself. This came from Thomas Cranmer, a Cambridge scholar, son of a Nottinghamshire gentleman, born in 1484; Cranmer had been a fellow at Oxford, and later a tutor to Anne Boleyn. Cranmer's plan was that Henry should send messengers to all the universities of Europe, asking the question: Is the pope competent to allow a man to marry his deceased brother's widow? Of course the answers made no difference, for Henry had his own answer ready. In 1532 Henry, accompanied by Anne Boleyn, paid a visit to Francis; Francis apparently advised Henry to take affairs into his own hands and promptly to marry Anne, and to let the pope rave. Henry took this advice, chiefly because it was what he wanted to do anyway. The marriage was performed between November 1532 and January 1533. Very fortuitously Archbishop Warham died at this time, and Henry replaced him by Cranmer, who he knew would support him. In January, 1533, Parliament passed a bill abolishing all appeals to Rome in matters of marriage or of those things that pertained to an ecclesiastical court. This naturally made the archbishop's court supreme, and Cranmer forthwith elected to try the question of the legality of the king's marriage to Katharine.

Katharine refused to appear to plead her case. Cranmer, basing his decision upon the opinions of the universities, declared the marriage illegal. Henry's marriage with Anne was immediately made public, and soon she was crowned amid great magnificence at Westminster. She was twenty-six years of age, and Henry was forty-two.

In September Elizabeth was born, and an Act of Succession was passed settling the crown on the children of Henry and Anne. Mary was thus ignored. The words of the act were carefully chosen in order to offend as little as possible the friends of Katharine. The coronation of the queen, the birth of Elizabeth, and the passage of the Act of Succession forced the pope's hand, and he threatened Henry with excommunication; in addition Spain was threatening to take a hand in the matter, but could not do so because of the unsettled state of affairs in that country. Henry therefore went his own way and things smoothed themselves out.

The Famous History of the Life of King Henry the Eighth.
The Play

Historic Time: 1520-1534.
Dramatic Time: 7 days.
Place: England: London, Westminster, and Kimbolton.
Purpose: The fickleness of a prince's favor.
Date of Composition: 1612.

Once again Shakespeare has gone to Holinshed's *Chronicles* for the source of most of the material of a play. Certain critics believe that the poet got some of his information from Cavendish's *Life of Wolsey* and some from Hall's *Chronicle*, but there is very little contained in those works that might not equally well be obtained from Holinshed. For the fifth act of the play Shakespeare very evidently used material from Foxe's *Actes and Monumentes of the Churche* (1563).

A great amount of argument has been made also concerning the authorship of the play, some critics claiming that Shakespeare wrote the entire play, a second group maintaining that he collaborated with Fletcher, and still a third group thinking that Shakespeare had nothing to do with the play whatever. To each his argument. So far as we are concerned here, since the matter cannot be proven from contemporary evidence, and since for so long this play has been included in Shakespeare's historical group, we will leave the arguments to others and proceed to study the play as so many thousands have done before, as being truly one of Shakespeare's. To most Shakespearean students the play is Shakespeare's, and that is the end of it. If anyone believes it is not, let him throw it out. Before doing so, let him read carefully Swinburne's *Study of Shakespeare*. Then, if he wishes the other side, let him read Spedding's argument, in *The New Shakespeare's Society's Transactions*, 1874.

Henry VIII is one of the least unified of Shakespeare's plays. Samuel Pepys once said of it that it was "made up of a great many patches", and in this he is correct. The dramatic critic will tell you that a good drama must be built around a central incident, that this incident must be the development from preceding events, and that the denouement that follows from this incident must be logical. If that definition is important, then this play is not good. As Pepys said, *Henry VIII* is simply a series of episodes, many of them entirely unconnected one with the other. At the beginning of the play the action and characters are grouped around Wolsey, but his part in the action ends with the third act and he passes from the scene. In the fourth act the central element is the coronation of Anne Boleyn, who never emerges as a prominent character but remains always in the background, and with the death of Katharine, who up to the third act had divided the interest of the action with Wolsey. Cranmer appears for the first time in the fifth act, and then he monopolizes the interest. In the earlier part of the play too much attention is paid to Buckingham, who is by no means one of the chief characters. The fall of Buckingham, the fall of Wolsey, the trial and death of Katharine, the rise of Cranmer, the marriage of Anne Boleyn, followed by her coronation, and the birth and christening of Elizabeth are all more or less unrelated incidents incorporated in the action of the play without any effort on the part of the playwright to weave the various plots together as he usually does in others of his plays having more than one plot. There is no unity of action, of actor, of time; the only unity existing is that of place, and that is here unimportant.

At no time in the play do we feel that Henry is an outstanding character. Unlike Richard III, who dominates the action, or Henry IV, who shares his prominence in *Richard II* with the ill-fated king, King Henry VIII appears throughout the scenes of this play as a character but not a personality, a man whom we come to know only in the last few incidents of the drama. No effort is made to commend him to us. We see his faults and shortcomings more clearly than his virtues; his sensuality, cruelty, and selfishness are revealed, but we do not so much despise them because the figure of Henry himself is so vague. If one single character stands out more than another it is that of the noble Katharine, whose calm dignity and resignation are ably described. Dr. Samuel Johnson considers her portrayal great; "the meek sorrows and virtuous distress of Katharine," he says, "have furnished some scenes which may be justly numbered among the greatest efforts of tragedy." But Henry stalks through the play, leaving us very little memory of strength or weakness save that for his selfish desire he is willing to sacrifice a devoted wife.

We are introduced to the action of the play by a conversation between Norfolk and Buckingham descriptive of the scenes enacted recently at the Field of the Cloth of Gold. Immediately we discover the discontent and hatred of the nobles toward the great Wolsey, especially that of Buckingham, who intends to air his complaints before the king, feeling secure of his own position. But squarely in the midst of that security appears

Brandon with a warrant for Buckingham's arrest, and the duke knows his end has come. The Buckinghams were of too noble an origin, and were therefore always dangerous to the peace of mind of their kings.

Next we see the council chamber. Henry is now devoted to Katharine. Nothing is too good for her. We learn too of her distrust of the great cardinal, whom she suspects as being hostile to those in whom her chief interest lies. We listen to the trial of Buckingham, and notice the absence of the defendant. He is doomed before the trial begins.   ,

The plot begins to thicken when next we see a party being given at York Place, to which Anne Boleyn (spelled *Bullen* by the poet) is an invited guest. The king butts in, disguised as a roisterer, and when his sensual eyes rest on the fair Anne, Katharine's doom is sure. Somehow we know that without reading further. Shakespeare may have obtained the material for this scene from the *Life of Wolsey*, by George Cavendish, Wolsey's gentleman-usher, who was present at the entertainment mentioned here. The party occurred on the 3rd of January, 1527.

The first scene of Act II records the end of Buckingham; the duke was tried on May 13, 1521, before seventeen of his peers, presided over by the Duke of Norfolk; he was executed on Tower Hill on May 17 following. Except for the fact that this scene contains some fine poetry it is entirely useless dramatically, save perhaps to show the ruthlessness of Wolsey. Immediately after we see the last of the duke, we get the first rumor of the approaching divorce proceedings against Katharine. In the next scene developments toward the divorce are rapid; armed with opinions from all the universities of Europe, Henry is ready to push his purpose to the limit. One short scene shows Anne Boleyn honored by the king with title of marchioness, a scene that shows Anne to very good advantage, by the way, and next we see the full pageantry of the divorce trial in Black-Friars.

Katharine indulges in one plea for justice here, and apparently seeing its uselessness, in dignity she withdraws, refusing to remain for further humiliation. She takes occasion, however, once more to speak her mind to the haughty cardinal, upon whom she places the blame for her trouble. After

she has left the hall each of the various churchmen undertakes to clear himself of responsibility concerning Katharine,
and Henry realizes that he is making little progress. He feels,
however, that things will be different when Cranmer returns.

Upon Katharine's refusal to be tried by an English court,
Henry sent the two cardinals to her to persuade her to relent.
She naturally is suspicious of them, but later, realizing the
hopelessness of her position, she relents and tells them to do
what they wish. All these scenes serve chiefly to portray better
the admirable character of the queen.

The next scene is one of the best in the play. We begin to
see the end of Wolsey not far off. He was guilty of double-
dealing with the king, for though he pretended to favor the
divorce, yet secretly he was opposed to it, and conducted a
clandestine correspondence with the Pope in an effort to postpone any action on the case. In addition he had accumulated
a tremendous fortune through his office with the purpose in
mind of applying it toward securing for himself election to the
papacy. It is an account of this that Shakespeare represents as
having accidentally been included in the papers the king had
examined. The king in the scene leads him on, giving him
enough rope wherewith to hang himself, very much after the
manner of Henry V when that monarch trapped the Duke of
York. But his letter to the Pope had come into Henry's hand;
that was too much. He was guilty of treason. The end comes
swiftly. Wolsey is placed under arrest by Surrey at the order of
Henry, and a list of the charges recounted to him. Holinshed
gives a list of the charges:

1. First, that he without the kings assent had procured to be a
legat, by reason whereof he took awaie the right of all bishops
and spirituall persons.
2. Item, in all writings that he wrote to Rome, or anie other
foreign prince, he wrote *Ego & rex meus*, I and my king: as
who would saie that the king were his seruant. . .
3. Item, he without the kings assent carried the kings great seale
with him into Flanders, when he was sent ambassadour to the
emperour.
5. Item, he without the kings assent sent a commission to sir
Gregorie de Cassado, knight, to conclude a league betweene the
king & the duke of Ferrar, without the kings knowledge. . .

7. Item, that he caused the cardinals hat to be put on the kings coine. . .

9. Item, that he had sent innumerable substance to Rome, for the obteining of his dignities; to the great impouerishment of the realme.

Then finally when Wolsey recognizes that he has lost irreparably the favor of the king, he discards his haughtiness and the hypocrisy which he had so long practised, and becomes sincere. It is then that he first enlists the sympathy of the reader. He is told by Cromwell that Sir Thomas More has been chosen Lord Chancellor in his place, and that Cranmer has been made archbishop of Canterbury. Actually Sir Thomas More became chancellor on October 25, 1529. Cranmer was made archbishop on March 30, 1533. On April 12, 1533, Anne Boleyn was openly acknowledged queen and plans for her coronation were made. When Wolsey is told by Cromwell that Anne Boleyn was publicly accepted, the broken cardinal recognizes that it is she who has caused his fall. "All my glories in that one woman I have lost forever", he says. But he is not bitter against the king; he wishes still that he may prosper. His farewell speech is one of the finest things in the play:

> Let's dry our eyes: and thus far hear me, Cromwell;
> And, when I am forgotten, as I shall be,
> And sleep in dull cold marble, where no mention
> Of me more must be heard of, say, I taught thee;
> Say, Wolsey, that once trod the ways of glory,
> And sounded all the depths and shoals of honor,
> Found thee a way, out of his wreck, to rise in;
> A sure and safe one, though thy master missed it.
> Mark but my fall and that that ruined me.
> Cromwell, I charge thee, fling away ambition:
> By that sin fell the angels; how can man then,
> The image of his Maker, hope to win by it?
> Love thyself last: cherish those hearts that hate thee;
> Corruption wins not more than honesty.
> Still in thy right hand carry gentle peace,
> To silence envious tongues. Be just, and fear not:
> Let all the ends thou aim'st at be thy country's,
> Thy God's, and truth's; then if thou fall'st, O Cromwell,
> Thou fall'st a blessed martyr! Serve the king;

And prithee, lead me in:
There take an inventory of all I have;
To the last penny, 'tis the king's: my robe,
And my integrity to heaven, is all
I dare now call mine own. O Cromwell, Cromwell:
Had I but served my God with half the zeal
I served my king, he would not in mine age
Have left me naked to mine enemies.

The next event in the chronicle is the coronation of Anne
Boleyn. The coronation actually took place on June 1, 1533.
Amid great pageantry the affair is consummated, but we see it
only through the eyes of "gentlemen". Aside from the historical narrative, the scene is of little importance dramatically,
in great contrast to the great scene that immediately follows.

Katharine, the "dowager-princess", is sick. Her good friend
and gentleman-usher, Griffith, recounts to her the death of
Cardinal Wolsey. Actually, Wolsey died five years before Katharine, but dramatically it is very fitting that she should hear
of his death as she herself is about to die. Capucius, ambassador from the Emperor Charles, comes to visit her, by whom
she sends a letter to the king, a letter full of pathos and very
touching. She begs the king to deal gently with young Mary,
and wishes him "a little to love her for her mother's sake,
that loved him, heaven knows how dearly." Also she would
have the king to see that her women are well cared for, and
that the men of her service be taken care of. She closes:

Remember me
In all humility unto his highness:
Say his long trouble now is passing
Out of this world; tell him, in death I blessed him,
For so I will. Mine eyes grow dim. Farewell,
My lord. Griffith, farewell. Nay, Patience,
You must not leave me yet: I must to bed,
Call in more women. When I am dead, good wench,
Let me be used with honor: strew me over
With maiden flowers, that all the world may know
I was a chaste wife to my grave: embalm me,
Then lay me forth: although unqueened, yet like
A queen, and daughter to a king, inter me.
I can no more.

In the fifth act for the first time Cranmer is introduced into the drama, and at the same time we are informed of his being encompassed with many enemies. The action in Act V passes immediately from one scene to another, without any break in continuity. The birth of Elizabeth is announced. Cranmer is summoned by his enemies to the council chamber, is kept waiting like a menial at the door, and is rescued by the king himself. Henry at last asserts himself, and wins from us something of respect at last. By virtue of the king's ring Cranmer survives, and the way is paved for the final great scene of the play, the christening of the baby Elizabeth. Actually, however, Elizabeth was christened on September 10, 1533, at Greenwich; it was not until 1544 that Cranmer was summoned to appear before the council.

The play closes with Cranmer's panegyric to Elizabeth's greatness, prophesying her glorious reign:

> This royal infant—heaven still move about her!—
> Though in her cradle, yet now promises
> Upon this land a thousand, thousand blessings,
> Which time shall bring to ripeness: she shall be—
> But few now living can behold that goodness—
> A pattern to all princes living with her,
> And all that shall succeed: Saba was never
> More covetous of wisdom and fair virtue
> Than this pure soul shall be: all princely graces,
> That mould up such a mighty piece as this is,
> With all the virtues that attend the good,
> Shall still be doubled on her: truth shall nurse her,
> Holy and heavenly thoughts still counsel her:
> She shall be loved and feared: her own shall bless her;
> Her foes shake like a field of beaten corn,
> And hang their heads with sorrow. Good grows with her;
> In her days every man shall eat in safety,
> Under his own vine, what he plants, and sing
> The merry songs of peace to all his neighbors:
> God shall be truly known; and those about her
> From her shall read the perfect ways of honour,
> And by those claim their greatness, not by blood.
> The bird of wonder dies, the maiden phoenix,
> Her ashes new create another heir
> As great in admiration as herself,

So shall she leave her blessedness to one—
When heaven shall call her from this cloud of darkness—
Who from the sacred ashes of her honour
Shall star-like rise, as great in fame as she was,
And so stand fixed. Peace, plenty, love, truth, terror,
That were the servants to this chosen infant,
Shall then be his, and like a vine, grow to him;
Wherever the bright sun of heaven shall shine,
His honour and the greatness of his name
Shall be, and make new nations: he shall flourish,
And like a mountain cedar, reach his branches
To all the plains about him. Our children's children
Shall see this, and bless heaven.

CHAPTER XII

Conclusion

The events of John's reign occurred slightly over a hundred years after the coming of the Conqueror, but the spring of the action of the play, *King John*, lies in the conditions arising from the Norman Conquest. The first William could never have realized in his wildest imagination the far-reaching influence of his ambition. However, the narrative of events in English history from William I to Elizabeth is the story of England's relations with France, all dating back to the coming of the Norman duke to assume control of affairs and to establish a new dynasty in England. The fortunes of this family of rulers furnished Shakespeare a theme for his series of plays.

To some readers the historical plays of Shakespeare may appear inferior to the tragedies and comedies in dramatic power, interest, and quality. This, however, is not necessarily true. From the standpoint of stage presentation the chronicles have held their own in popularity through the years. The history of the English stage reveals the fact that the chronicles have been offered as often as other types of Shakespearean drama, have been received with as much acclaim, and have been performed by as great artists. To the capable actor the historical play provides excellent opportunity for exercising talent. No character in the whole of Shakespeare is more clearly drawn than that of Richard of Gloucester, riding rough-shod over his victims to the throne itself. No humorous character in the comedies provides more mirth than fat old Falstaff, prince of wags and master of puns. No public hero is found in Shakes-

peare with more effective appeal than Hotspur, the warrior
who would turn a river from its course because its tortuous
windings robbed him of territory he had not yet captured.
Shakespeare's picture of Richard III yields nothing to that of
Macbeth. If one desires the portrait of a brave patriot, Faulconbridge is the equal of Brutus. Henry V is as strong, John and
Henry VI as weak, respectively, as Coriolanus and Lear. Falstaff's wit is as the sunlight to the beams of the moon when
compared to Touchstone or Launcelot or Feste. Only in respect
to the women of the chronicle plays do we find the characterization weak in comparison. There is no Imogen, no Corde-
lia, no Desdemona, no Miranda. But Richard's Isabel is a lovely
queen, beautiful in her grief as she parts from her husband.
No woman elsewhere in Shakespeare expresses mother-love so
beautifully nor so sorrowfully as Constance, mourning for her
lost son. And through three entire plays the spirit of Margaret,
she-wolf of France, ill-fated queen to a hapless king, holds
sway over the entire action. No other woman in Shakespeare
is honored by her appearance in more than five acts. Men
and women throng the pages of the historical plays, all of
them living characters, as real and vivid as those of any of
the great tragedies or comedies. Truly, the historical plays
need no apologist; they speak for themselves.

If the chronicle plays are interesting dramatically, they are
equally so from the standpoint of history, itself. Shakespeare
has taken a cross-section of English record and has presented
it so vividly, has peopled it with such vital characters, that
the period itself has come to mean more to the common man
and woman than any other similar span of years in Britain's
entire history. He has pictured the whole array of events in a
manner truly striking, from the pageantry of the autocrat
John to the demagoguery of the genial Tudor Henry, and by
so doing he has also presented the full flowering of knighthood as it blossomed and finally scattered its petals toward
the end of the fifteenth century.

A study of the chronicle plays, too, reveals many interesting
excursions made by the dramatist from the straight road of
historical truth, each deviation being eternally justified by the
dramatic effect gained thereby. Sometimes two events occur-
ring actually two or more years apart are represented as

happening on the same day, and often one character is made to take the place of two historical personages. Years are sometimes added to children to furnish them maturity and subtracted from adults to render them children. Good men are represented as evil, and wickedness is converted to piety to suit the occasion. But all to a purpose.

A number of such warpings of historical truth occur in *King John*. Arthur, a young man of sixteen years, is made in the play into a mere child, with a child's actions and thoughts. By doing this the dramatist has given us a gentle, lovable boy for whose evil fate the whole world mourns. Dramatically Arthur, the lad, is vastly more touching a figure than ever the real Arthur could have become. Shakespeare's Arthur is one of the most charming children of all his many creations. The boy's mother, too, lived longer in Shakespeare's imagination than in life, for actually she died a year before Arthur was captured by John. But think of the dramatic loss a strict adherence to truth there would mean! Her last speech in the play justifies every liberty taken with facts.

John of Gaunt is one of the most eloquent figures in *Richard II*, but he was not so in life. The dramatist has taken a rather mediocre man, whose negative tendencies were more toward evil than toward good, and has made of him one of the noblest characters in the whole series of plays. His absence from *Richard II* would be a distinct dramatic loss, with his nobility of nature and patriotic eloquence. Had his tongue throughout the play been a "stringless instrument", there would have been a distinct poetic void.

More drastic still was the poet's transformation of Richard's queen. She was at the time of the events of the play just ten years old; as such she was of no dramatic use. But as a woman, a devoted wife, she adds the beauty of poignant grief to the pathetic end of the hapless Richard, and her devotion is evidence to us of Richard's personal charm. Her farewell to her ill-fated husband forms some of the most beautiful poetry of the play.

Hotspur is an outstanding example of historical adaptation. Excellent character that he is in his own right, his chief function in *Henry IV* is that of a foil to Prince Hal. Bring it about that Hotspur is recognized as possessing all these manly attributes of the national hero, and let Hal overthrow Hotspur; naturally Hal falls heir to his victim's idealization. Shakespeare uses a magic brush in his delineation of the fire-eating warrior, making of him one of the best drawn characters in the series. But all of the glorification of Hotspur is simply an added glorification of Hal. To accomplish his purpose, to make Hotspur a rival of Hal's the poet had to reduce Hotspur's age by twenty years, and had to warp history in other ways, for historically the two never came together in hostile conflict. We are indebted to the imagination of the playwright for one of the most dramatic episodes in all drama. And Falstaff at Shrewsbury is priceless. We could not possibly dispense with him there. The dramatic effect of Hotspur's characterization more than equalizes any guilt for having manhandled historical accuracy.

But one of the most effective adaptations of character is that of Richard of Gloucester. He is introduced first as a fire-eating young warrior, doing yeoman's service in saving the life of the hardpressed Salisbury, at a time when actually he was two years old. And from that moment through three plays his personality makes itself very much felt. History has never borne witness that Richard himself killed young Edward Lancaster or his father, Henry VI. But think how effective his subsequent wooing of Anne becomes with such a background as that! History does not concur altogether with Shakespeare in picturing Richard's deformity. He was malformed, perhaps, having one shoulder higher than the other, and it may be that he walked with a limp, but it is doubtful that he was the hunchback so ably depicted by the poet. But Shakespeare's figure of the man at whom the dogs barked as he passed by, whose arm was withered and whose back was bent, is vastly more dramatic than the Richard whose picture appears so normal in the commonplace histories of the times.

The wooing of Anne historically was a matter of two years, but in the play the action requires but a half-hour. A great deal is gained by this dramatically. In the first place, it was a matter of dramatic economy. The more important effect of the telescoping of the action, however, is to show the power of the dynamic personality of the ambitious duke. We have explained elsewhere Anne's apparently ignominious surrender, but actually it was a master stroke of dramatic genius, for it portrayed better than a hundred pages of prosaic history the overpowering personality of the man. If Richard could win Anne in two years against such odds as he had to overcome, he could do it equally in an afternoon. And the dramatic effect was tremendously enhanced thereby.

Shakespeare brought Margaret back from her father's home in Anjou to appear twice in *Richard III,* when the record shows that she never returned to England once she left it after Henry's downfall. But Margaret's presence is one of the really great touches of the play. True, she seems scarcely a flesh and blood figure, but more of an apparition, coming and going as she pleased, unseen and unmolested by her enemies; yet her appearance adds much to the dramatic effect of the play. The curses she utters form somewhat of a skeleton for the subsequent action, prophecies that inevitably must come true. Her spirit—the spirit of Nemesis—hovered over the events that transpired in those troublous times, and her absence would have been a most distinct loss to the effect of this great chronicle. Truly the poet did well in summoning the bold-spirited queen once again across the waters of the English Channel.

Thus the art of the great dramatist has seized upon the salient points of matter-of-fact history and by the application of poetic imagination has enlivened the characters and events of a bygone era so that they become for us the living and moving elements of a great scene. Shakespeare has metamorphosed the dry lines of history into human documents, quickened them into human figures, so that for three hundred years they have kept their flesh and blood outlines and continue to move before us with the vividness of yesterday. The poet has set the figures of great Englishmen on so splendid a stage that they personify finally and for all time the characteristics of the English race. Doing this too in the earliest period of his productiveness, he has more than earned for himself first place among all those who have created the glories of English literature. The pages of the ten historical plays are surely a testament to his gifted genius.

INDEX